Mainstreaming

Edited by Effie Papatzikou Cochran

Case Studies in TESOL Practice Series

Jill Burton, Series Editor

Teachers of English to Speakers of Other Languages, Inc.

Typeset in Berkeley and Belwe
by Capitol Communication Systems, Inc., Crofton, Maryland USA
Printed by Kirby Lithographic Company, Inc., Arlington, Virginia USA
Indexed by Coughlin Indexing Services, Annapolis, Maryland USA

Teachers of English to Speakers of Other Languages, Inc.
700 South Washington Street, Suite 200
Alexandria, Virginia 22314 USA
Tel 703-836-0774 • Fax 703-836-6447 • E-mail tesol@tesol.org • http://www.tesol.org/

Director of Communications and Marketing: Helen Kornblum
Managing Editor: Marilyn Kupetz
Copy Editor: Marcia Annis
Cover Design: Capitol Communication Systems, Inc.

ISBN 0-939791-97-8
Library of Congress Control No. 2001 135532

Dedication

This volume is dedicated to Edith Brenner Everett, the feisty member of "The Giraffes," who, for more than a quarter of a century, has been sticking her neck out in support of the public education of language minority students—her heroes.

And to Mariah Natasha Leontopoulou-Cochran—the youngest bilingual member of my family.

Table of Contents

Acknowledgments

I wish to thank all the authors who worked hard, shared generously, and waited patiently for this book to come out. We are grateful to Series Editor Jill Burton; to Marcia Annis, our copy editor; and to Marilyn Kupetz, TESOL's managing editor, for their professional guidance, encouragement, and caring throughout the process.

Series Editor's Preface

The Case Studies in TESOL Practice series offers innovative and effective examples of practice from the point of view of the practitioner. The series brings together from around the world communities of practitioners who have reflected and written on particular aspects of their teaching. Each volume in the series will cover one specialized teaching focus.

◈ CASE STUDIES

Why a TESOL series focusing on case studies of teaching practice?

Much has been written about case studies and where they fit in a mainstream research tradition (e.g., Nunan, 1992; Stake, 1995; Yin, 1994). Perhaps more importantly, case studies also constitute a public recognition of the value of teachers' reflection on their practice and constitute a new form of teacher research—or teacher valuing. Case studies support teachers in valuing the uniqueness of their classes, learning from them, and showing how their experience and knowledge can be made accessible to other practitioners in simple but disciplined ways. They are particularly suited to practitioners who want to understand and solve teaching problems in their own contexts.

These case studies are written by practitioners who are able to portray real experience by providing detailed descriptions of teaching practice. These qualities invest the cases with teacher credibility, and make them convincing and professionally interesting. The cases also represent multiple views and offer immediate solutions, thus providing perspective on the issues and examples of useful approaches. Informative by nature, they can provide an initial database for further, sustained research. Accessible to wider audiences than many traditional research reports, however, case studies have democratic appeal.

◈ HOW THIS SERIES CAN BE USED

The case studies lend themselves to pre- and in-service teacher education. Because the context of each case is described in detail, it is easy for readers to compare the cases with and evaluate them against their own circumstances. To respond to the wide range of language environments in which TESOL functions, cases have been selected from EFL, ESL, and bilingual education settings around the world.

The 12 or so case studies in each volume are easy to follow. Teacher writers describe their teaching context and analyze its distinctive features: the particular demands of their context, the issues they have encountered, how they have effectively addressed the issues, what they have learned. Each case study also offers readers practical suggestions—developed from teaching experience—to adapt and apply to their own teaching.

Already in published or in preparation are volumes on

- academic writing programs
- action research
- assessment practices
- bilingual education
- community partnerships
- content-based language instruction
- distance learning
- English for specific purposes
- gender and TESOL
- grammar teaching in teacher education
- intensive English programs
- interaction and language learning
- international teaching assistants
- journal writing
- literature in language teaching and learning
- teacher education
- technology in the classroom
- teaching English as a foreign language in primary schools
- teaching English from a global perspective
- teaching English to the world

◈ THIS VOLUME

Mainstreaming entails teaching through and about a host culture while recognizing the heritage cultures and languages that learners bring with them. Writers in this volume celebrate the knowledge, skills, and practices of primary-, secondary-, and tertiary-level students whose first languages are not English, and examine procedures and processes that have supported such students as they learn to be full participants in the host culture.

Jill Burton
University of South Australia, Adelaide

INTRODUCTION

Becoming Full Participants in the Host Culture

Effie Papatzikou Cochran

Although initially controversial, *mainstreaming* has now been recognized as a sound academic concept and practice because "language learning and content learning are simultaneous processes in the human mind . . . [with] most language learning tak[ing] place while the learner is concentrating on learning something else" (Cochran, 1992, p. 2). Language learning being a lifelong process, it is very difficult "to define a point at which language learning is basically complete and content learning can begin" (Cochran, 1992, p. 2).

Mainstreaming takes many forms in schools and programs in various parts of the world. It arises from a concern to do justice to nonnative English speakers throughout their schooling from elementary to secondary, further on into college, and beyond. But what all mainstreaming efforts have in common is the commitment to bringing language minority students into regular, integrated content classes with their native-English-speaking peers. Effective learning and support are key objectives here—support that is not limited to the language minority student but directed as well at the mainstream teachers whose classes these students eventually reach.

The chapters in this volume reflect successful experiments with mainstreaming ESL students throughout the English-speaking world. In addition to descriptions of U.S. programs, examples of mainstreaming programs in Australia, Canada, and New Zealand are included. The first five chapters cover primary and secondary programs. The others primarily describe postsecondary or graduate programs.

❖ OVERVIEW

The volume as a whole offers a variety of models of mainstreamed programs. The authors' approaches are quite different, but there are common threads that connect their several notions of mainstreaming: a fervent desire for inclusiveness on behalf of the English language learner, a desire for equal educational and social opportunity, and a compelling argument for seeing, as Clegg (1996) once put it, "ESL learners as less 'different'" (p. 5).

There are more particular insights that emerge from these chapters as well, of course. One of these is the clear importance of a variegated immigration pattern to the development of well-articulated mainstreaming programs. It is clearly no accident that some of the most serious and successful mainstreaming programs reported in this collection come from institutions located in parts of the world that are dominated by across-class, high-volume immigration, such as the provinces/states of British Columbia, Canada (Greenholtz, chapter 9), and Victoria, Australia (Arkoudis & Davison, chapter 5). One can logically conclude that when mainstreaming efforts appear to have been less successful, it is not because mainstreaming does not work, but rather because the special adaptations that need to be made, absent a well-educated and numerically significant immigrant population, were not made.

Yet these cases also make clear that, as desirable as these common threads are by way of societal background, they are not a *sine qua non*. Mainstreaming works anywhere, under virtually any conditions. ESOL learners as a class are among the most motivated students in an educational system. We should not be surprised that this is the case. What more motivating innovation in a person's life can there be than being plunked down into a foreign culture in which one cannot speak the language, or cannot use it with sufficient ease in reading and writing to function professionally, and realizing, "Self—it's sink or swim!"

It is the schools and the teachers, therefore, that are the only real variables in the mainstreaming equation. So when we see the kind of districtwide institutional orientation toward "wholeschool" ESL that Barnett reports (chapter 1), or the devotion and creativity of Osgood (chapter 4) and Upton (chapter 7) (to single out two of the teachers in this collection whose personal and professional commitment to mainstreaming is most transparent in their writing), we realize that we are in the presence of the single, supremely simple solution to what some so misguidedly conceive as the ESL problem. The solution is teachers who will build their teaching on their students' needs and institutions that will listen to and support those teachers. This does not mean dumbing down instruction (for one of every motivated student's needs is the need to be inspired, to be lifted beyond what they thought they knew); it just means that teaching is everything. Whoever said "the faculty are the university" was right (see Rosenthal, chapter 6, and Gareis, chapter 10).

Finally, every one of these chapters makes clear that mainstreaming is an absolute necessity without which the educational process cannot process. Whatever legitimate need there may be for self-contained and sheltered classes early in an ESL student's academic career, as Milambiling (chapter 2) correctly asserts, mainstreaming is still the goal. And it is, in fact, more than the goal: It is also the process by which ESL learners do most of their learning. One used to hear non-ESL-trained academics talk about mainstreaming as one option among many, of dubious, or at least untested, merit. The enormous variety of mainstreaming contexts and programs represented in this collection, and the natural ease with which virtually all of them have been integrated into the life of their schools and colleges, show that an optional attitude toward mainstreaming is no longer an option for any serious educator.

◈ MAINSTREAMING IN PRIMARY AND SECONDARY SCHOOL SETTINGS

Based on her involvement and experience with a number of ESL mainstreaming efforts in South Australian primary and secondary schools, Barnett (chapter 1) writes of ESL as a "wholeschool endeavor." She reports on programs that have been successful not only in teaching ESL to their target populations in mainstream environments, but even in bringing entire schools into cooperative participation with the ESL task. She offers powerful testimony to the fact that mainstreaming at its best is no different from all education at its best.

Milambiling's report on an elementary school mainstreaming program in the United States (chapter 2), discusses how the Iowa program brings English language learners into daily contact with native-English-speaking students. The program seems to perform successfully, though the author would prefer a somewhat longer period in self-contained classrooms for newly arrived learners. This chapter bears testimony to the truth that—given caring, committed, and creative responsiveness to the local situation—ESL students can be mainstreamed in any school environment.

McKay and Lewis (chapter 3) describe a Roman Catholic School near Auckland, New Zealand, with a multicultural and linguistically diverse student body. They outline New Zealand's general guidelines for integrating ESL students and give some grade-specific details about the school's ESL options. The chapter points out that the arrangements made by a particular school depend on influences such as national or regional education policies, the nature of the school population, and the school's ethos.

Osgood vividly describes her "Challenge Program" in chapter 4. With it, she "attempts to initiate" every fourth- through eighth-grade ESL beginner who enters her Pennsylvania school district. Eleven startling pedagogical revelations emerge from her classroom "challenges."

The ways in which a "secondary college" in Victoria (one of the most linguistically diverse states in Australia) has sifted through its available program options to develop an integrated ESL program is the focus of Arkoudis and Davison (chapter 5). The program is characterized not only by the integration of ESL and content areas in materials and methodologies, but also by outstanding curricular and policy support from the state educational system of which their secondary college is a part.

◈ MAINSTREAMING IN POSTSECONDARY SETTINGS

Rosenthal (chapter 6) describes the transitional ESL program in a medium-sized state university in New Jersey, in the United States, as one of several examples of how that institution prepares limited English proficient (LEP) students to enter the mainstream. LEP students whose native language is Spanish are concurrently enrolled in the college's Spanish-speaking and ESL programs. The university's transitional program allows nonnative English speakers to enroll in introductory general education courses taught in English by ESL-trained content-area faculty. Rosenthal is explicit about the as yet unsolved problems her program faces and freely solicits helpful suggestions from readers. Her analysis of these problems is highly illuminating in its specificity and for its applicability elsewhere.

As he outlines the development of an academic bridge program at a medium-sized U.S. university in Indianapolis, Upton (chapter 7) describes a program that provides at least 10 bridge, sheltered, and paired or "adjunct" courses for its ESL students. Most remarkably, the program operates without a budget, thanks to its success in persuading university faculty and staff to share this program's duties, along with their regular responsibilities.

Lesikin (chapter 8) provides a detailed model for a paired general education

(GE) course in U.S. racism, classism, and sexism at a New Jersey university. Further, this carefully thought-out mainstreaming program provides fine points that others could fruitfully adapt to help students attain the academic competence needed for success in their mainstream college courses. The critical message of the chapter is how intensively the ESL instructor has to prepare in order to be able to help her students through their paired GE counterpart courses.

Greenholtz (chapter 9) describes a postsecondary Canadian program that is part of an exchange program between the University of British Columbia (UBC) and a university in Kyoto, Japan. UBC's Academic Exchange Programme has a number of features that deserve to be closely studied. The program is intentionally flexible so that the needs of early mainstreamers and experienced students still in need of academic sheltering can be met.

Gareis's chapter 10 is unique in two respects: It is the only report in this collection that focuses on oral communication, and it is the only chapter to describe ESOL mainstreaming efforts within a postbaccalaureate degree program of a City University of New York (CUNY) college. The course, entitled "Speech for International Business Students," has been taught since the spring of 1998. A welcome innovation is the concentration on oral communication and the coalescing of ESOL techniques around that as a primary goal, especially in light of the importance of oral proficiency for success in the business workplace.

The assessment of educational outcomes rests at the heart of the mission of any pedagogical enterprise. It allows us to ascertain the extent to which our mission, purposes, and goals are being reached, makes it possible to carry out midcourse corrections, and is a crucial tool for enhancing our own effectiveness. Patkowski (chapter 11) describes the efforts at outcomes assessment in a college-based ESL program whose fundamental mission is to prepare students for the academic mainstream. This chapter is included here as a guide to all who need to conduct outcomes assessment in their schools and offers practical suggestions applicable to all grade levels. Patkowski's detailed statistical analysis was conducted over a 3-year period in his urban college's ESL program.

In chapter 12, Cochran describes a pilot survey of her U.S. urban college's mainstream faculty. It questions them about their academic expectations of the nonnative-English-speaking students in their courses. This study also attempts to detect hidden attitudes on the part of these university professors toward ESL students. The chapter offers tables, insights, and suggestions for improving the questionnaire should readers desire to send something similar within their own university system.

◈ CONTRIBUTOR

Effie Papatzikou Cochran is an associate professor in the Department of English at John Jay College of Criminal Justice of the City University of New York. She is a teacher educator, author of numerous articles, and editor of the 1992 CUNY handbook, *Into the Academic Mainstream: Guidelines for Teaching Language Minority Students.* Her article on Greek diglossia appeared in *International Journal for the Sociology of Language* in 1997. She is coeditor of *Issues in Gender, Language Learning, and Classroom Pedagogy* (2001), commissioned and published by NJTESOL-NJBE in collaboration with Bastos Educational Publications.

PART 1

Primary and Secondary School Programs

CHAPTER 1

From the Margins to the Center: ESL as a Whole School Endeavor

Jennifer Barnett

❖ INTRODUCTION

In schools where every class has bilingual learners, the ESL program needs to become a whole school endeavor. It needs to shift from the margins of the school to the center. I take this position after many years of observing ESL programs in schools, and I justify it here on the basis of a recent three-school case study.

In the schools I observed, everyone was involved in the ESL program: staff, students, and the local community. They were involved not simply as support for ESL students, but as participants in developing a fully plural community. ESL as a whole school endeavor addressed the ESL learning task, as well as the conditions in which it took place—all those factors in the school environment that affected ESL learning. These efforts aimed to improve factors such as attitudes to difference, cultural diversity in subject content across the curriculum, opportunities for engaging socially and talking across cultures, home-school relations, and assessment practices. Different factors were prioritized, depending on the school and how well it already supported the ESL learning task. Nevertheless, the overall focus was consistently on improving conditions of learning.

The whole school endeavor built on existing mainstream programs in three important ways. First, it involved teams of people working together collaboratively. Second, it involved an inclusive whole school ethos. Third, it involved open, active exchanges between family and school. These three features are described in some detail in the body of this chapter. Then, taking collaboration as the key feature, I have suggested some practical ideas for working toward ESL as a whole school endeavor in other settings.

❖ CONTEXT

ESL programs in South Australian schools generally understand the ESL learning task as having three related components:

1. learning a new language
2. learning a new culture
3. learning how to attend school and achieve academically in the new setting

In schools where ESL is marginal, sometimes only the first component is widely acknowledged, whereas in schools where ESL is mainstream, all three components are acknowledged. However, it is only in schools where ESL is a whole school endeavor that a collaborative and integrative approach to the threefold learning task is made possible.

The three schools discussed in this chapter all saw ESL as a whole school commitment. They were located in the poorer suburbs of Adelaide, the capital city of South Australia, and catered to the first 7 years of schooling. In these schools, as many as 25% of 5-year-olds walked through the classroom doors with very little experience of English or of mainstream culture. One school's enrollment was about 70% Vietnamese heritage,[1] with families who had been settled in the community 1–20 years and who consistently spoke Vietnamese in the home. In another school, the enrollment was predominantly of Italian heritage, but with parents who were the children or grandchildren of immigrants and who spoke Italian only with older members of the family. In the third school, there was a shifting mix of communities, and the school enrollment included 15 different heritages.

Within each community, there were many variations in language use and cultural practice. In some homes, no English at all was spoken, and the cultural practice replicated that of the family heritage as much as was possible in an Australian setting. The children entered school fluent in a heritage language (or sometimes several) and competent in many social practices relevant to the heritage culture, but with barely a word of English and little experience of the dominant culture. In other homes, some family members spoke to the children in an English colored by the heritage language, and others spoke a form of that language colored by English, with correlating variations in cultural values, beliefs, and social practices. The children received a bilingual, bicultural upbringing as part of a new and developing community. They entered school with a fair command of English but did not receive much academic English language extension in the home over the years of schooling. In some homes where the parents spoke in English, the primary caregiver was an elderly relative who spoke only the heritage language. In such cases, the child was usually more orally proficient in the heritage language than in English and developed only a limited and chiefly passive use of English before entering school. This was particularly true of only children and eldest children. All these variations meant that students had variable ESL learning tasks, which teachers needed to identify and specifically facilitate.

Entering a Reception (kindergarten) class at age 5, the children experienced one of several possible ESL learning environments and types of exposure to English:

> Where there are very large numbers of the same language students in Reception, those students talk that language among themselves, often not taking any notice of the teacher. This is the case where there are, for example, 17 Vietnamese students in Reception. Bilingual school assistants are very supportive, and there is some excellent linking with family, but the ESL exposure is limited. (ESL teacher in a school with high Vietnamese enrollments)

---

[1] I use the word *heritage* in preference to *background* because the latter privileges the school over the home and community. Although the children's linguistic and cultural experiences may be background to the teacher and school, they are not background to the children and their families.

Where there were small numbers of the same language students in Reception, those students had more exposure to English, and teachers tended to establish routines providing a balance between the social support offered through other L1 speakers and the ESL learning opportunities offered through English speakers.

New arrivals who entered the middle and upper primary years as ESL beginners not only had to learn all the English language up to the level of their peers but also the school culture and previous curriculum as well as the peer group culture outside school. In addition, their task in the mainstream classroom was made harder because there was typically considerably less collaborative, hands-on, and visual activity in the middle primary years. Students who were ESL learners in Reception often also found difficulty with this.

> Once we remove the visuals and scaffolding at Year 4, we find ESL students struggling. In particular, the teachers say they can't inference [sic] meanings. These are typically students whose parents speak English with them, but who have primarily been raised by an Italian-speaking grandmother. In Junior Primary writing, the teachers do lots of joint construction, but this stops in Year 4. There is the assumption that the children know all about that. (ESL teacher in a school with high Italian enrollments)

This teacher's comments highlight the shifting nature of the ESL learning task, which changes as the learner progresses through school. In other words, learner need for support recurs because of changing classroom demands and continuing limited access to English outside school.

The ESL learning task does not have static goals, but ones that shift as learners progress through school, and the demands of school become ever more complex. Consequently, for individual learners, what counts as ESL content is the gap between what they know and what they need to be able to do in their life circumstances as the years go by. It is the movable gap between (a) their current ESL proficiency and (b) whatever English language and cultural proficiency is required to achieve learning outcomes appropriate to their academic level and to engage successfully in social interactions appropriate to their age. Teachers' understanding of the changing learning task can be a major factor in whether or not students achieve their academic goals and their English language potential.

Although Australia acknowledges itself to be a multicultural nation, many teachers have little experience of plurality prior to joining schools such as these. Consequently, not all children's cultural and linguistic resources are recognized or built upon in classrooms. Curriculum policy, too, tends to privilege monolingual multiculturalism, a policy that positions bilingual learners as "other": It is a view which identifies a standard culture for the society, a kind of monolithic unanalyzed norm which tolerates diversity as though it were a condition of otherness (Lo Bianco, 1999).

However, in the schools described here, with their high populations of bilingual learners, cultural and linguistic diversity was the norm, and all staff were obliged to respond to this norm. All of these schools had a strong concern for multiculturalism, for equity in curriculum access, and for affirmative action to assist students to achieve their learning potential. These were the key concerns that generated ESL as a whole school endeavor.

◈ DESCRIPTION

This chapter is based on work I did for two reviews of the school ESL programs provided by different education authorities in South Australia. *Review of the English as a Second Language (ESL) Program* (Barnett, Walsh, Pangyres, & Hender, 1998) was undertaken for the state government, whereas *Review of ESL Provisions in South Australian Catholic Schools* (Barnett, 1999) was for the state Catholic education authority. Both involved a survey of all schools with an ESL enrollment and included visits to 12 metropolitan primary schools. During this review process, I came across several instances of schools working toward ESL as a whole school endeavor. It appeared to be a powerful and effective process requiring more detailed attention than the commissioned reviews could give.

I wanted to find out more about the characteristic features of ESL as a whole school endeavor and to draw out the factors that supported it, as well as some practical ideas for application elsewhere. I therefore decided to develop a case study based on further analysis of the review data. I first identified three schools that offered a whole school ESL program. Two were in the Catholic system and one was in the government system. The next step was to sift again through the survey and site visit data. Although the survey data firmly established the mainstream approach to ESL and the involvement of staff, students, and the local community, it did not provide sufficient detail. So I turned to the site visit interviews with principals and deputies, ESL coordinators and teachers, classroom teachers, a range of support staff involved in the program, and students. There was a wealth of detail here, backed up by field notes from brief classroom visits and by written timetables and teacher programs.

What follows is a composite of the findings that were replicated or paralleled across the three schools. This provides a picture of the characteristic features of ESL as a whole school endeavor in those schools and the factors that shaped its development.

◈ DISTINGUISHING FEATURES

In each of the three schools, ESL as a whole school endeavor grew out of the *ESL in the Mainstream* (Education Department of South Australia, 1991) professional development program. This was originally developed in South Australia and has since been redeveloped and sold internationally. This program emphasized collaboration between ESL specialists and class teachers and the involvement of ESL specialists across the curriculum. One teacher describes a working week representative of all three schools:

> Approximately 25% of my time is spent in parallel teaching when students work on similar tasks as mainstream students but with more assistance with writing and comprehension tasks. About 30% of my time is used for collaborative teaching, assisting ESL students in mainstream classes. Another 25% of my time is spent doing withdrawal teaching. During this time I work with students on special programs to address particular learning needs, for example, building word knowledge and correct word usage. It is also an opportunity for them to use oral language. The remaining time is used for support teaching, for example, providing models to assist students with

writing (genre structures), [and] providing scaffolding for ESL students to ensure they are able to understand/complete tasks. (ESL teacher)

This sort of program was very much valued:

> The modeling and skill of our ESL teacher provides an excellent professional structure for all of our teachers. The constant reinforcement of being inclusive, of supporting all learners in their language, the importance of literacy and good literacy practice, are supportive structures for our teachers in all classes. . . . You cannot put a price on the importance of this role and the value for teachers in their ongoing and onsite professional development. (School principal)

As in this school, ESL specialists in the other case study schools were all taking on professional development roles, supporting teachers as much as learners. They were also developing other human resources, supporting parents and peers to take on new roles. This in itself is not particular to ESL as a whole school endeavor, but it was certainly a historical prerequisite in these three schools.

What does seem to be inherent to ESL as a whole school endeavor is a complex of three features:

1. the deliberate fostering of team approaches in supporting bilingual learners

2. the development of practices to support inclusive experiences of schooling

3. the deliberate fostering of interactive home-school relations

These three features are described below, drawing on what was common among the case study schools.

Team Approaches

As a key feature of ESL as a whole school endeavor, each school had an ESL management team for strategic planning and facilitation, and ESL support teams for supporting bilingual learners. The ESL specialist was central to both kinds of teams. He or she no longer worked alone, often in adverse conditions, but was a respected member of a whole team of people working collaboratively toward a shared goal.

The management team consisted of the principal or deputy principal, the ESL specialist(s), and the staff member coordinating the literacy program, and was the core planning team for whole school strategies such as

- multicultural and antiracist education

- principles to guide the allocation of staff support to students

- facilitating the participation of parents in their children's schooling

A key role the management team played was to establish and guide ESL support teams for learners, teachers, and parents. This included encouraging community involvement and manipulating the timetable to allow for collaborative planning. Because of demands on senior management, the day-to-day practicalities of management were carried out by the ESL specialist(s) and often the key literacy teacher. The main tasks for the management team were to work out appropriate ESL support teams for individual students and groups of students in different mainstream classes, to assist these teams to develop relevant and cohesive programs, and to monitor learner progress.

At the whole school level, everyone was a part of an overarching ESL support team and contributed through positive attitudes and language use, and through nonracist and antiracist behaviors. Students contributed through friendship, through the buddy system, through peer and cross-age tutoring, and through cultural exchange. Teaching staff contributed through inclusive curriculum, targeted support, and by modeling intercultural respect. Management contributed through inclusive administration, affirmative action for parent groups, and by providing time and resources to support the process as a whole. Members of the community contributed through participation in management and curriculum development, through class-room support, parent support, and cultural events.

Within this broad affirming framework, a number of small teams supported individual learners or groups of learners. These were established and facilitated by the ESL management team, which responded to the observations and concerns of class teachers and ESL teachers.

The ESL support team for each class always included the class teacher, so in one sense there were as many ESL support teams as there were classes with ESL learners. The team often included volunteers from the community, parent body, and student body. However, most of the other staff members of the teams were stable, being chiefly drawn from

- teacher assistants (some bilingual)
- adaptive education teachers, who support all students with learning difficulties
- teacher librarians
- community language teachers

Each support team was matched appropriately to a class in terms of students' ESL proficiencies, the expertise of the class teacher, and available resources. In one school, support teams divided up the year levels so that support people could develop strategies suitable for a particular age group.

The following factors were particularly important for the success of team approaches:

- the involvement of the principal or deputy in the management team
- time allocated for planning and coordination among all team members
- a strong equity ethos in the school
- a history of staff collaboration in the school
- individual teachers with skills in working collaboratively (or interested in developing such skills)

Team approaches enabled staff to support each other in their skills development, to provide a cohesive program for ESL development, and to focus individually on fewer students, thereby becoming more familiar with their learning needs and more able to support them appropriately. They also helped the class teacher to develop inclusive practices across the curriculum.

Inclusive Schooling

Each of the three schools had, over time, been reviewing curriculum and classroom practices to determine if they were inclusive of all students and thereby supportive of the ESL learning task. Where necessary, they had replaced or adapted these practices according to principles of inclusive schooling. They were thus able to offer an education that represented all students; valued a wide range of cultural experiences, knowledge, and viewpoints; and responded to the diverse language, cultural, social, and academic resources students brought with them to school. Classroom practices were adjusted to address the needs of all students and included culturally diverse subject content and assessment that acknowledged the ESL learning task. These case study schools made a strong commitment in their school policies to principles of cultural inclusivity. Key aims stated in these policies were to

- foster acceptance of all children
- support one another's cultures, sharing and affirming each other's traditions
- break down language barriers

Teachers learned to reconstruct the mainstream curriculum so that it was accessible and relevant to students, while still maintaining its general themes and standards. They did this by means of culturally inclusive and language-conscious classroom practices such as the following:

- incorporating students' cultural heritages in subject content
- deliberately building up the cultural and linguistic resources that are taken for granted in mainstream curriculum
- building on students' prior knowledge and experience
- teaching content across the curriculum, making meanings clear through realia and visual aids
- modeling and scaffolding language use and cultural practices
- providing opportunities for oral activity through small-group and one-to-one interactions
- offering firsthand experiences of Australian social situations (e.g., shopping, public transportation, swimming pools, and museums)
- offering a vibrant whole school program in a local community language
- ensuring targeted inclusion in extra curricular activities (e.g., debating, drama, sport, camps, and assemblies)
- providing opportunities for children to talk about curriculum content in their first language
- setting up work groups of students with similar cultures

One of the schools also developed language awareness studies, which were designed, as Bourne (1997) suggests, to take "account of the resources bilingual children bring to knowledge about language, legitimating and extending their knowledge, and recognising their achievements" (p. 60).

In addition, all three schools firmly resisted the pressures on the classroom language curriculum of national literacy benchmarking conducted through reading and writing only. They maintained and continuously developed a focus on oral language, valuing oral language as a key phase in the ESL learning task.

Because these inclusive practices required all staff to develop appropriate professional skills and resources, the characteristic team approaches were valuable in supporting them to acquire the new skills that were needed. The teams facilitated professional development and optimized staff expertise.

Interactive Home-School Relations

The third distinctive feature of ESL as a whole school endeavor was the development of interactive home-school relations. This was decidedly a two-way process. Schools wanted to hear and discuss the views of parents on their children's education and to have parents involved in classroom activities and in program development. They also wanted to be able to keep parents properly informed about their children's school-based learning, to discuss it with them, and to involve them in the process. In the two schools where there was a fairly homogeneous bilingual population, it was possible to establish quite viable processes for parent involvement in the management of the school. For example, the school with a high population of Vietnamese-speaking students had negotiated with community leaders to discover the most suitable way to increase parent involvement. Together they had established a subgroup of the school board, consisting entirely of Vietnamese-speaking parents. The principal participated in the subgroup with the aid of an interpreter, and at full-board meetings, he helped representatives of the subgroup to air their views effectively. In the school where the community was more diverse, the principal's pursuit of interactive home-school relations resulted in the provisions of guidelines for the school board and the introduction of interpreter support at school board meetings. This subsequently led to community involvement in assisting teachers to develop inclusive classroom programs and to locate appropriate materials.

In all three schools, parents felt confident enough to visit the school, to participate in their children's learning, and to contribute to classroom program development. Interactive home-school relations were difficult to establish and maintain in multicultural communities where principals and teachers spoke no language other than English and where few parents were able to bridge the cultural and linguistic barriers without help. In the past, there was government funding for home-school liaison staff, but there was very little of that at the time of this study. Consequently, interactive home-school relations were generated through locally constructed schemes, which aimed to develop good, two-way communication and strong parent participation in the school.

In addition, the schools used several or all of the following strategies to assist the parents of bilingual learners to participate in mainstream schooling:

- informal support of parents through parent-teacher interviews (the ESL teacher took part in these when possible, interpreters were made available when possible and desirable)

- a regular program or occasional information evenings held with interpreters to help parents understand curriculum and classroom activities and to help their children with schooling

- the translation of school newsletters, surveys, consent forms, and report cards (when finances permitted)

- a network of long-term school parents supporting new school parents and their children

- mothers' groups from different communities meeting at the school (morning teas)

- ESL programs run on the school premises for parents

- cultural events staged at the school with parent involvement

For each school, further developing interactive home-school relations continued to be one of their major concerns. As such, relationships are liable to be particularly fragile and adversely affected by frequent changes in the staffing of poorer schools, as well as by their limited resources.

◈ PRACTICAL IDEAS

The success of ESL as a whole school endeavor had a lot to do with strong leadership in the three schools, strong advocacy for ESL, and an inclusive and caring school ethos. It also had a great deal to do with the skills of the ESL specialists, not only in supporting ESL students but in supporting their teachers in developing inclusive curricula. Building optimum conditions took time and effort, which had to be consistently maintained, especially in the face of staff transfers and ESL funding cuts.

Schools need practical ideas to develop the required conditions. In addition, advocacy for ESL has to come not only from ESL specialists but from senior management and classroom teachers. It is built up through increasingly close association with bilingual learners and their families, through progressive understanding of the issues, through active concern for child rights, and through collaborative reflection and action. Advocacy often involves breaking down resistance, and acknowledging underlying fears, bringing them into the open, and addressing them. Very often what staff most need is a way of working together to understand and become comfortable with whole school ESL issues.

A very practical way that the three schools in this case study did this was to identify one particular issue in ESL support and try to respond to it collaboratively, making use of team approaches, principles of inclusive schooling, and interactive home-school relations. This focused collaboration was a powerful element in moving toward ESL as a whole school endeavor. Three whole school strategies are briefly explored below as vehicles for this process that could be used elsewhere.

Respond Collaboratively to ESL Issues in the Reading Program

One issue that concerns all schools with bilingual learners is that commercial reading programs are frequently not suitable for developing ESL learning skills. This is partly because they assume so much mainstream cultural knowledge and partly because they assume a readership that is fluent in English. Teachers tend to find that progression through a reading program is often heavily dependent on a hierarchy of knowledges (e.g., word knowledge, cultural knowledge, and grammatical knowledge). These are knowledges that ESL students may not yet have developed in

English, even though they have done so in their heritage language. Thus, some ESL students are labeled as poor readers, even though the reality is that they simply have more ESL learning to do. In addition, the progression of texts often does not provide the necessary scaffolding and recycling of language to assist ESL learning.

An issue for ESL as a whole school endeavor, therefore, is how to establish a reading program that develops not only reading skills but ESL. As a first response, teams can collaboratively evaluate their existing programs in relation to the ESL learning task. They might ask questions about the texts themselves and also about their own methods of working with text. Does the reading program:

- include texts that are culturally meaningful to the students, in which they can see themselves and their families?
- guide students to select books at their own level?
- expose students to different genres of writing that they can use as models for their own writing?
- include texts relevant across the curriculum that will allow students to build up field knowledge and vocabulary through the program?
- ensure plenty of oral interaction around the text?
- build knowledge of word meaning rather than taking it for granted?
- build cultural understanding rather than taking it for granted?
- recycle new vocabulary, language patterns, and cultural understandings?
- provide for explicit teaching of unfamiliar grammar?
- emphasize visual memory as well as sound-letter relationships (for students whose pronunciation does not help them with sound-letter relationships)?
- build on bilingual reading skills?

Teachers may find that they can improve the reading program against all of these criteria, especially with the help of teacher librarians to select multicultural, language-conscious, and visual publications in all fields of knowledge. Together they can seek out resources that provide for different levels of English proficiency in relation to one content area so that a single resource-based activity can be set for students to participate in at their own level. Teams can also step up community involvement in classroom activity, as well as cross-age and peer tutoring and the use of bilingual teacher assistants (where possible). This means that more children can have one-to-one oral interaction around a text. Teams can also set up parent workshops on the reading program, guiding parents to support their children's reading at home, even if their own English language is not fluent.

Respond Collaboratively to ESL Issues in Teaching New Content

A second issue that teams can address collaboratively is working out what sorts of content class teachers ought to make explicit when introducing a new topic in a subject area. Like the commercial reading program, everyday teaching often assumes a cultural knowledge and knowledge of word meanings that the ESL student may not yet have. However, teachers find it very hard to be constantly alert to their assumptions because assumptions do have a way of making themselves invisible. Below is an example of mistaken assumptions we surely all have made ourselves.

The class was given a simple labeled diagram on how wheat grows. The teacher slowly gave a time-sequenced explanation of the diagram several times. Photographs of wheat growing and being harvested were displayed. Vocabulary such as *stubble* and *tiller* (i.e., *side stem*) was explained. The students were then asked to write about the diagram. One ESL child wrote half a page, which included the following sentences:

> *Wheat is a grain that flower grow to make a beautiful flower.*
>
> *Tillers a size of a stem.*
>
> *Finally, in summer it has stubble and ready to be harvested.*

Clearly, the student not only missed out on an opportunity to learn new content but missed out also on an opportunity to enlarge her vocabulary meaningfully. With 28 children in the class, how could the teacher have avoided this? What practices might have helped? By sharing their experiences, teams can collaboratively come up with answers such as these:

- Never assume knowledge of the key words in a topic.

- Write all key words on the board (fluent English-speaking students can do this as part of an initial brainstorm at the start of a topic and again after new terms have been introduced).

- Use concrete realia (e.g., flour, an ear of wheat, and a loaf of bread).

- Explicitly teach words that sound the same (e.g., *flower/flour*).

- Write sentences alongside visuals so that the child can use new vocabulary correctly.

- Have key word preparation in pairs before writing (for ideas, sequencing, and spelling).

- Provide for selected learners a skeleton of key words to be used in a written task.

- Have a buddy, a parent, or an extra staff member available to the child when introducing new content or undertaking content writing.

Respond Collaboratively to ESL Issues in Assessing Written Tasks

One final example of the sorts of issues that teachers can collaboratively address is how to assess accurately what children can do in their written English. With a literacy benchmarking approach, it is all too easy for ESL learners to be assessed as poor writers, when the reality is that they merely still have some way to progress in ESL. Multiple perspectives on assessing writing are needed. In the first instance, writing needs to be assessed in terms of what the child can do as a writer and as an ESL learner. Take the following example.

The child started school 8 months prior, at age 5. She was beginning to use routine social language in oral interaction but relied heavily on an attentive listener to make meaning from other things she said. Her writing reflected this. She wrote the following sentence using the opening phrase *on the weekend,* which was written on the board.

> *On the weekend I my Mum blai me fou bslitedhmnows is.*

This sentence can be written out in correct spelling as:

> *On the weekend I my Mum buy me for beautiful? new shoes.*

And can be rephrased more grammatically as:

> *On the weekend my Mum bought some beautiful new shoes for me.*

Teachers collaboratively reflecting on this piece might come up with the following notes on what the child can do as a writer:

- understand the required literacy task and respond meaningfully
- know how to write some words independently (e.g., *Mum*)
- have a concept of what a word is
- know that spaces separate words
- know that a sentence starts with a capital and ends with a full stop
- know that the written form should reflect the sounds heard
- hear some initial sounds and write them (e.g., *blai* [*buy*]) and *fou* [*for*])
- be able to find in the classroom words that she needs and copy them (e.g., *weekend*)
- write what she hears through the sound system of her first language

Following that, teachers might then think about what the child can do as an ESL learner:

- understand the teacher's instructions
- know the basic subject-verb-object sentence structure of English (subject: *I my Mum*; verb: *blai*; object: *bslitedhmnows is*)
- know that sentences can begin with a statement of circumstance
- use a possessive form: *my Mum*
- understand the relationship between *for* and *me*, but has not yet learned the word order required in English
- know that *buy* may have an indirect object, *me fou*, without yet knowing its most usual position in everyday English
- construct a sentence through the grammar of her first language

Using this dual perspective, teachers can readily support each other to see that the child is not struggling with writing itself. She is not a slow learner. On the contrary, she is demonstrating a high learning curve in her first year of schooling and her first year of learning English. But this can only be recognized through a dual perspective on assessment. Teachers may also add other perspectives. For example, in science reports and historical recounts, content learning must also be assessed. And when writing on a computer, assessing information technology skills will add a fourth perspective. By involving Vietnamese speakers from among students, staff, or parent groups, teachers could add yet another perspective in terms of assessing this student's transferred linguistic and cultural resources. Different teachers will emphasize different perspectives, and by collaboratively assessing a variety of written pieces they can bring them together and think about how they should be weighted. This may well reduce teacher anxiety and generate whole school strategies for assessment.

◈ CONCLUSION

In the three schools discussed in this chapter, the ESL program involved all staff, all students, and the local community as well. The ESL program extended beyond simply addressing the ESL learning task to addressing the conditions in which ESL was taught and learned. The schools were each characterized by strong school leadership, ESL advocacy, and a whole staff commitment to achieving the best possible learning outcomes for all students.

Because of its focus on the conditions of ESL learning in mainstream settings, ESL as a whole school endeavor has the potential to bring about change in overall school cultures and communities, going well beyond the time and place of the ESL program itself. The priority on supporting staff and parents, as well as bilingual learners, means that everyone has the opportunity to learn what they most need to know to facilitate the ESL learning task and to improve the experience of schooling for bilingual students.

As a process, ESL as a whole school endeavor represents a unified and integrated strategy for facilitating the ESL learning task. It takes the ESL program from the margins to the very center of schooling.

◈ CONTRIBUTOR

Jennifer Barnett is a senior lecturer in TESOL at the University of South Australia, in Adelaide. She teaches in bachelor of education, master of education, and doctoral programs, focusing on ESL in the mainstream and factors affecting second language acquisition. Her current research concerns the nexus between ESL and literacy development in mainstream schooling and in indigenous education programs.

CHAPTER 2

Good Neighbors: Mainstreaming ESL Students in the Rural Midwest

Joyce Milambiling

◈ INTRODUCTION

In the wake of Proposition 227 in California and discussions in other states about what kinds of instructional settings are best for ESL students, there is still no definitive answer. Educational solutions for these students must take into account a variety of factors, including the length of time the students have lived in the country of resettlement, whether they are immigrants or refugees, and what educational experiences they have had before coming to the United States. Even if schools consider these and other factors, the resulting programs usually need to be adjusted on a regular basis and sensitive to local contexts in order to meet the evolving needs of students, teachers, and institutions.

This case study reports on an elementary school (K–5) in rural Iowa, in the United States, and how the mainstreaming of ESL students, mostly Bosnian refugees, was designed and implemented. The study looks at this particular elementary school and the surrounding community in terms of the social and organizational framework in which language use is situated. This perspective is essential because decisions about which languages are used in school, how languages are taught, and how students are grouped for instruction all have social and political origins and repercussions. The first part of the title of this article, "Good Neighbors," reflects the importance of becoming something other than a stranger in this setting and how the active learning of English from the time immigrants arrive in the area is strongly associated with their becoming members of the larger community.

The mainstreaming of ESL students in U.S. schools is a process that warrants honest and critical examination, especially in light of global demographic and economic trends. Immigrant children are aware of the need to speak English in their new environment, resulting, for many of them, in no longer being able to communicate in the home language and to connect with the cultures and traditions of their families. This phenomenon is troubling to some researchers (Fillmore, 2000). Whether or not ESL students lose their L1, the pressure put on them to speak, read, and write English makes becoming accepted in U.S. schools and communities a combination of intense linguistic as well as social effort.

◈ CONTEXT

Cedar Falls/Waterloo and Immigration

The metropolitan area of Cedar Falls/Waterloo is located in northeastern Iowa, in the upper midwest region of the United States. These two communities are situated north of Iowa City and northeast of Des Moines, the capital of the state. Jasper Elementary School is located in a town on the outskirts of Cedar Falls. In many ways, the community in which Jasper Elementary is located is a typical midwestern one, with a population of predominantly Western European ethnic origin. Cedar Falls is home to the University of Northern Iowa, which has a student body of 13,000, consisting mostly of Iowa state residents. The industries in the area are primarily agriculture and heavy manufacturing.

Compared with other states, Iowa is not a magnet for immigrants. The total population of the state as reported in the 2000 census (U.S. Census Bureau, 2000) was just under three million, with a legal immigrant population of 113,500 (approximately 3.9%). Since 1990, an average of more than 2,500 new immigrants per year has entered the state, arriving mostly from Mexico, Vietnam, and the former Yugoslavia. Immigrants from the latter two countries have predominantly been classified as refugees and are therefore immediately eligible for federally reimbursable benefits, such as medical and social services. During the fiscal year ending July 1997, international immigration accounted for close to 65% of the state's population increase. As is true for many midwestern states, the increasing numbers of immigrants, particularly with Hispanic backgrounds, offset the decreasing numbers of European American residents, a trend that has been called the *browning* of the Midwest (Huffman & Miranowski, 1996).

A major employer of immigrants in the Cedar Falls/Waterloo area is the meatpacking industry. IBP, Inc., has a large pork processing plant in Waterloo. During the past 15 years and until very recently, the workers recruited to work at these plants have been Hispanic and Southeast Asian. During recent years, one researcher estimated the number of Bosnian refugees who have come to work at the Waterloo IBP plant to be more than 3,000, many of whom were recruited specifically to work in meatpacking. Other meatpacking plants in Iowa employ large numbers of primarily Hispanic immigrants (Grey, 1997). Meatpacking is an industry that has evolved to require fewer skills than in earlier years, and it has a reputation for being the most hazardous industry in the United States. Low pay and difficult working conditions have led to a high turnover of employees, with local residents (nonimmigrants) less and less willing to work at such jobs. Immigrants, including refugees, accept the jobs largely because their employment options in the United States are usually very limited. The immigrant workers often bring families that include school-aged children (Grey, 1997).

The community in which Jasper Elementary is located is not a diverse one, and being accepted and fitting in are both important social aspects, probably more so than in communities where there is greater diversity. The nonimmigrant population has to make some adjustments to accommodate the changing environment, but the immigrant population is under greater pressure to fit in, and anything that can be done to help them adjust and to nurture acceptance among all residents is valuable. The fact that the newcomers are mostly refugees is also crucial for understanding the importance of their finding a niche in this new environment—Iowa is now home, and their options for returning to their native countries are limited, if not nonexistent.

The result of these changing demographics is that Iowans have been brought face-to-face with people who have different languages, customs, religions, and childrearing habits. Immigrants are welcomed to the state for their contribution to economic development, but they may be regarded with suspicion or indifference once they arrive and even for years afterward. Efforts to eliminate negative perceptions of immigrants in Iowa and other states in the Midwest have met with some success, but there is still room for improvement.

ESL

One of the burdens of school districts that have large numbers of ESL students is that they must establish programs to accommodate the students. These programs require trained ESL teachers and very often instructional aides who speak the students' L1(s). This is difficult enough to accomplish in states such as New York and Illinois, which have large concentrations of ESL students, but it presents even greater problems in regions that have smaller immigrant populations and less experience educating students who are not proficient in the language of instruction.

In the Waterloo area, the number of school-aged children who require ESL services has grown tremendously due to the recent influx of Bosnian refugees. There are also Hispanic immigrants attending local schools, but their numbers have remained relatively stable. A pair of articles in the local newspaper that appeared in late 1997 illustrate the growth of the limited-English-proficient population (Stanton, 1997a, 1997b). In 1996, there were approximately 50 students who required ESL services, whereas in December 1997, there were more than 400. By April 2001, according to the Waterloo Community School District (central office staff, personal communication, April 2001), the number had climbed to more than 800.

One of the biggest problems with providing ESL instruction for immigrant children is finding money for teachers, aides, and facilities. Students are counted in September, and the budget is determined for the following year, not the current one, based on that number. This often results in a year-long shortfall, even longer if the same increase in numbers of students happens the following year. Some of the money for personnel and facilities comes from local sources, but the district has applied for state and federal funds.

◈ DESCRIPTION

Since the spring of 1997, Jasper Elementary School has received a significant number of students who speak little or no English, adding up to about 25% of the total number of students each year. The data gathered for this case study consist of interviews with teachers, administrators, and other school staff about the social and academic climate of the school and analysis of school records. Those interviewed were also asked how they feel about the ability of ESL students to cope in mainstream classrooms.

District Level

In the Waterloo Community School District, four elementary schools have been designated to receive ESL students who need special services, and each of these schools currently has room for 70–100 ESL students. Jasper Elementary is one of these four schools.

School Level

The current model of mainstreaming immigrant students evolved from the arrangement during the 1997–1998 school year, when ESL students were in self-contained classrooms. They were separated not only during class time, but also, voluntarily, during lunchtime, recess, and before and after school. The decision to integrate the ESL students into the larger student population arose from the belief that something had to be done to help them become part of the wider school community. As the principal stated, "We had to do something socially and give them services at the same time." One of the key aspects of this decision was to reduce class size; this was done by decreasing the number of interpreters by two and acquiring an additional teacher. This extra teacher is placed at the level that has the greatest need and would benefit from a reduction in class size. During the 1998–1999 school year, this teacher was placed at the combined fourth-/fifth-grade level, but during the 1999–2000 school year, this teacher was placed at the second-grade level. All the classes in the school are now divided between two interpreters, who are available to those teachers, students, and parents assigned to them on an as-needed basis.

During the 1999–2000 school year, the total school population at Jasper was slightly less than 400, including 104 ESL students. Most of these ESL students were Bosnian (93), 9 were Hispanic, 1 was Vietnamese, and 1 was Albanian (whose parents read and write Serbo-Croatian). The school has three kindergarten classes; three first-, second-, and third-grade classes; and four combined fourth-/fifth-grade classes. ESL students are now placed in regular classrooms from the beginning of their schooling at Jasper.

The placement of students is based on a variety of factors, including the age and educational experience of the student, the number of students other than ESL students at that grade level who are receiving special education services, and the overall number of students at that grade level relative to the number of teachers available. If a student has previously attended Jasper, his or her teacher from the previous year is consulted during placement decisions. The wishes of parents in individual cases are also taken into consideration as much as possible.

Generally, Jasper offers ESL services to nonnative-English-speaking (NNS) students and native-English-speaking (NS) students with nonstandard needs in various groupings, depending on a student's grade level and availability of staff. The result is neither a traditional pullout structure, in which students are taken out of the regular classroom for special instruction, nor is it strictly a push-in arrangement, in which a specialist teacher (typically an ESL teacher) goes into a regular classroom. Rather, it is a flexible structure in which, in most cases, ESL students receive services (e.g., help with reading) alongside NS students who have similar needs. Sometimes an extra teacher goes into the room, and sometimes students change rooms, but ESL and NS students are, for the most part, affected in similar ways. Newly arrived ESL students, however, do receive intensive ESL services, usually on a one-on-one or small-group basis.

Individual Classes

Students are grouped within classes for instruction and special services. In kindergarten and first grade, ESL students are generally not grouped in any special way. The Title I teacher spends time in the morning in the first-grade classes doing guided reading, and the special education teacher goes into the first-grade classes and works with students who are designated special education and have Individual Education Plans.[1] According to one of the first-grade teachers, "At first grade and kindergarten, these [ESL] kids have it made because they're all learning the same thing." There is an interpreter available for the teachers at these levels, in case any of the Bosnian students has a problem or an extended explanation is needed in Serbo-Croatian. For the Spanish speakers, there are interpreters available from the central office, but they do not work in the school on a regular basis.

In the second grade, students who need special help (this includes ESL students as well as other students) receive instruction in language arts from one of the teachers in the morning. This arrangement was not anticipated at the beginning of the school year but soon became necessary. In addition to the new arrivals entering at this level, other second-grade students having difficulty with reading received this additional support as well. One of the interpreters works regularly with a reading group in the second grade. Even though she is there because of her ability to speak Serbo-Croatian, she also works with ESL students who speak other languages. The two interpreters said that they were happy with this kind of arrangement because they "get to know more kids this way; not just ESL, but all kids."

In the third grade, there is one designated ESL teacher, formerly a special education teacher, who works in the morning with students who have special educational needs (among them, five new ESL students). The other students at that level are divided between two other teachers during that time. The designated ESL teacher employs a variety of resources to help the new students and those ESL students and other students who need additional support in reading and other areas. She devises activities and uses materials that target a variety of learning styles, works with students on a one-on-one basis, solicits the help of student volunteers from the University of Northern Iowa, and calls on associates who work in the building to assist in her classroom.

In the combined fourth/fifth-grade classes, ESL and students with Individual Education Plans are divided among the four classes, with one class having as few as 3 ESL students and one having as many as 12, or a little less than half the class. The fourth/fifth-grade class with the most ESL students meets in the ESL-trained teacher's room and remains there for most of the day. It sometimes happens that the ESL students sit in a group by themselves, although it is more likely that there will also be non-ESL students in the group. The fourth/fifth-grade class teacher, who is certified

---

[1] An Individual Education Plan is written by a team of educators and a student's parent(s) and contains an agreed-upon set of goals to help the student achieve greater academic success in the general curriculum.

in ESL, listed the kinds of skills that she works on with ESL students, either one-on-one or as a group. These include basic survival vocabulary, such as their address and telephone number, and asking to use the bathroom. These skills are practiced at various appropriate class times and can take place during any subject discussion.

Use of Available Resources

During an interview, one fourth/fifth-grade teacher related how she and her colleagues make use of the Minnesota Migrant Resource Center. This center loans materials to teachers, even those working at remote sites. The materials can be used to reinforce content needed to meet the school district's standards and benchmarks. The hands-on materials can be used with all students, especially ESL and non-ESL students, who need more context for academic work. The materials include objects and pictures for bulletin boards and centers, song lyrics, worksheets, books, and other materials. According to the teachers, one advantage of working with the Migrant Resource Center is the availability of its trained staff, who make every effort to provide material requested by the teachers. The kinds of materials available from the Resource Center are often termed *supplementary materials* and are effective in the classroom teacher's quest to "enhance meaning and clarify confusing concepts, making lessons more relevant" (Echevarria, Vogt, & Short, 2000, p. 27).

One activity that is available to all students is the Accelerated Reader® program (2000), a computer-based program that motivates students to read and tracks their progress. Students choose a book that is part of the program from the school library, read it in school or at home, and then take a computerized test about the book. The test checks the students' basic comprehension of facts and events from the book. The computer program provides a test score based on the difficulty of the book and keeps track of the points each student earns. The teacher keeps these records and shares them with the school principal. The Accelerated Reader program is one component of a broad approach to reading called Reading Renaissance®.[2] This approach stresses regular reading practice, motivating students to read, and keeping track of their progress. All classroom teachers receive training in this technique.

◈ DISTINGUISHING FEATURES

It is important to emphasize that the ESL students described in this study are primarily refugees and, therefore, have certain needs that other immigrants might not necessarily have. Although nearly everyone who comes to a new country experiences some sort of culture shock, refugees from Bosnia and other war-torn areas often experience several kinds of shock. As a Bosnian case manager who works at the Iowa Bureau of Refugee Services noted, "Physically it's hard, technically it's hard, and emotionally it's hard" (Porter, 1998). The adult refugees need to settle in, learn the language, and find jobs quickly because they do not have the option of returning to

---

[2] Reading Renaissance® is the reading component of the Renaissance™ school improvement process. Renaissance Learning, the company that markets this process, provides seminars, sells software (including Accelerated Reader®) and other materials, and provides consulting services to the educational community. Their Web site is http://www.renlearn.com.

their home countries as do so many other immigrants. Although some of the refugee families have relatives already living in the United States who are available to offer family support (e.g., grandparents who can baby-sit), many do not.

Watchful Integration

Jasper Elementary School is distinctive in that it mainstreams students from the beginning of their schooling yet continues to provide them services as needed. It uses a kind of watchful integration rather than putting ESL students into mainstream classes and expecting immediate adjustment and comparable performance. Students attend this school because of the ESL and other services that are available to them and, thus, are given time and special help to develop the necessary academic and social skills to succeed in their new environment. If they were to go to another school in the district that did not offer these support services, they would be on their own to a far greater extent.

In support of this integration of students, interpreters are used efficiently and creatively in this school. The two interpreters are pleased with the roles they play at Jasper; they do not reside in any one classroom but are available to work in classes that need them as well as to make phone calls and home visits, and do paperwork. As they put it: "We have many teachers, many rooms." They also believe that immigrant students benefit from the integrated model that this school uses. They report that the immigrant parents are happy that their children are learning alongside NS children.

The result of the services offered at Jasper is that ESL students become socially integrated into the school, and this helps all of the students to accept diversity, according to one of the staff members. The teachers report that all of the students learn about their peers' holidays (e.g., Ramadan) as well as other details of one another's cultures and customs. When the process is reciprocal, teachers and other students can learn about where these refugee children come from and what they have been through, and the immigrant children can learn the things they need to learn to survive and succeed in the new country. At the same time, the ESL students are developing their academic skills and learning content matter alongside their peers, receiving extra support as needed.

Successful Performance First

Another aspect of Jasper Elementary is that students are not returned to their home schools until they have been performing solidly at their grade level for 1 year. These expectations for performance are often exceeded beyond everyone's hopes. During the 1999–2000 school year, for example, one of the fifth-grade ESL students was at the top of her class, and her third-grade sibling's performance was virtually indistinguishable from that of her NS classmates. The perception among the teachers and administration was that this would not have occurred had the ESL and other students been in separate classes.

Computer Familiarization

In addition to integrating ESL students with mainstream students, Jasper Elementary uses computer-based programs, such as Accelerated Reader (described earlier in this chapter) and Let's Go! Interactive (1995), a multimedia computer program designed to help students develop listening, speaking, and prereading skills. These computer programs are used to motivate students and give them extra practice in reading and other language skills. They also help ESL students become familiar with computers; this skill is vital to their future education.

Supporting Tolerance

Other services at Jasper Elementary have been instrumental in providing a place for ESL and other students to solve conflicts and discuss problems. The two associates who work in the planning room at the school reported that when the ESL students first came to the school, they used the planning room differently from other students; they were mostly sent to the room to discuss behavior problems that stemmed from their lack of familiarity with school policies and standards of behaving. These staff members have been trained to listen to the ESL students and to recommend solutions to their problems. During the 1998–1999 school year, there were several incidents on the playground in which non-ESL students would refer to the ESL students from Bosnia as "Bosnians," until the principal and other staff insisted that all students use each other's first names. This, they related, has resulted in a clear and consistent policy that has decreased, although not totally eliminated, ethnic labeling. They also remarked that when the ESL and non-ESL students were in separate classes, they did not bother to learn each other's names, but that now they not only know one another but are forming friendships across ethnic lines. One of the associates interviewed said, "Before it was 'us' and 'them.' Now it's much more 'we'."

Jasper Elementary School—One of a Kind?

This specific elementary school is distinct—as is every school—because of the composition of its student body, staff, and location in a particular geographical and social context. Other notable aspects include the integration of ESL students into the school and their preparation for mainstream academic work, the composition of individual classes, how teachers (including ESL teachers) are assigned at each grade level, the way interpreters are used throughout the school, and how closely the progress of each ESL student is followed throughout his or her attendance at school. Another significant aspect is that the school is working on a schoolwide federal Title I plan because of the generally low income levels among the families whose children attend, which means that there are more special personnel available to work with students.

◈ PRACTICAL IDEAS

Other schools can look to this case as an example of how one school has designed a program that makes a sincere effort to meet the social and academic needs of its total student population. Staff treat the body of students as an organic whole and employ a number of strategies to deliver effective instruction to an increasingly diverse group of students.

Consider Social and Academic Factors

Students coming to a new place with a new language have to adjust on many different levels. Gaining acceptance among their peers is often a long process for children, and they will need to succeed socially and academically in their new home as well. The school certainly has a responsibility for the academic part of this process, but the school can also play a key role in helping students adapt socially. Opportunities for students to get to know one another across ethnic and linguistic lines abound in the school setting, and students should be able to interact freely during different kinds of activities. One opportunity that was implemented at Jasper is to pair ESL and NS students for reading, which then opens the door for friendships outside the classroom. One of the reasons for the mainstreaming model that was implemented at Jasper was to short circuit some of the misconceptions that the students might have of one another by letting them get acquainted and learn to appreciate one another in and out of class.

Make Creative Use of All Available Resources

Computer programs such as those used at Jasper and the availability of supplemental materials through the Minnesota Migrant Resource Center are just two examples of the kinds of resources available to teachers. Teachers use technology and services in different ways and often find out about these from colleagues by word of mouth. Visiting other teachers' classrooms is a good way to see what others have found and how they use different materials and services.

Be Flexible

Flexibility is an invaluable quality for educators. In the context of Jasper Elementary School, teachers and administrators were flexible in how they grouped students as well as how they allocated resources. When experimenting with different arrangements, it is important to document the results from a variety of perspectives.

◈ CONCLUSION

The model of mainstreaming in which ESL students are integrated into classrooms with NS students from the beginning of their schooling should not be perceived as one that can be applied automatically in other settings, nor should it be seen as a leveling mechanism for linguistic and cultural diversity. Students at Jasper Elementary School are encouraged to value and draw from their own cultures but also to learn together and help one another on an everyday basis. The social context and attitudes of the participants are important considerations when deciding on an instructional model, as is having the necessary administrative and instructional resources with which to provide more individualized instruction to all students, not just to ESL students.

Personally, and in general, I am a proponent of bilingual education and sheltered models of ESL instruction. I believe that the L1 and culture of students should be used actively and be prominent in the education of ESL students for as long as possible. I am convinced that acquiring academic proficiency in an L2 takes a considerable amount of time, and that "very different communicative proficiencies

[are] required of children in school encounters, as compared to the one-to-one, face-to-face interaction typical of out-of-school contexts" (Cummins, 1984b, p. 17). I also believe that self-contained ESL classrooms are often the best environments for newly arrived students initially and, possibly, for longer periods to help them develop academic and linguistic skills and become comfortable in their new surroundings and with the new culture.

I was doubtful when I first heard about the integration of students at Jasper Elementary School; I was concerned that it was simply a new version of the old sink-or-swim programs prevalent in the United States during earlier periods of the country's history. I do not believe that this is the case at Jasper, largely because students are not left to succeed or fail on their own but, rather, are monitored closely and helped to succeed and to build on skills that they already have. They are given help in areas in which they need it and in this way are not treated any differently from any other student in the school who requires more time or different teaching techniques.

However, we should suspend judgment about Jasper's ultimate effectiveness until more data are gathered and, ultimately, until the ESL students who are there now have gone on to middle school, high school, and beyond. The long-term effects should be monitored not only for students who are in mainstream classes from the start but also for those who are in self-contained or sheltered classes. For now, all of the students' academic and social needs at Jasper are being considered on what seems to be an equal footing—they are all children first and ESL or non-ESL students second. This might not work in every setting, but it seems like a practical and useful approach in this one.

◈ CONTRIBUTOR

Joyce Milambiling is assistant professor at the University of Northern Iowa, in the United States, where she teaches courses in linguistics, teaching methodology, and other subjects for TESOL students. She does research in the areas of language teaching and learning, and is especially interested in implicit and explicit language policies.

CHAPTER 3

Mainstreaming in a New Zealand Multicultural School

Denise McKay and Marilyn Lewis

◈ INTRODUCTION

This case study describes the work of McAuley High School, a secondary school in Auckland, New Zealand, which has a range of new speakers of English. It shows how the school's philosophy of being concerned for each student's total development has led to an integrated academic and social program that helps ESL students adjust to regular school life.

The chapter starts by setting McAuley in the wider context of New Zealand's national provisions for new speakers of English. It then gives a brief profile of the local district. The school's programs are outlined in the context of national provisions, the local context, students' options, and the roles of teachers. The chapter also explains the principles that underpin the school's mainstreaming efforts and features that distinguish this school, even within the multicultural city of Auckland. Finally, it offers practical ideas that schools in other parts of the English-speaking world could implement.

◈ CONTEXT

The National Context

The New Zealand Ministry of Education has several provisions for assisting schools with large numbers of ESOL students and students with other special needs. To assess the needs of schools, the ministry collects data using various methods. For example, it categorizes all schools on decile scales according to the socioeconomic status (SES) of the district. This scale measures a number of indicators, such as total household income, the number of people living in a house in proportion to the number of bedrooms, parents receiving government support, and parents' occupational groups. Decile 10 is the highest SES level and Decile 1 the lowest. McAuley High School is categorized as a Decile 1 school.

Another basis for government support is students' competence in English. In its document, *ESOL Resourcing Information*, which is updated regularly, the Ministry of Education (1998) makes clear which schools are and which are not eligible for supplementary funding in this category. For example, schools are advised to "omit [from any funding application] any student who has already attended a New Zealand school for more than four years. It is expected that these students will have moved from the group with highest needs targeted by this resource" (p. 1).

However, a wider group of students than those fitting the 4-year rule is recognized; these are students who come from backgrounds where languages other than English are spoken. The same ministry document refers to a national school population of 62,000 students whose families have arrived from other parts of the world: the Pacific Islands, Asia, the Middle East, Africa, and Europe. Of these students, some are considered to fall into a special funding category. Quota refugee students who arrive in New Zealand through the official refugee program spend 6 weeks at a center that happens to be located in the same area of the city as McAuley High School.

New Zealand secondary schools provide a range of organizational options for students arriving from non-English-speaking countries. These are, in ascending order of students' English language competence:

- a separate program for up to a year

- a separate program for a few weeks

- partial integration throughout the year

- complete integration with in-class support from an ESOL/bilingual teacher

- complete integration with partnership teaching

- complete integration from the start

One further source of assistance is available nationally. The New Zealand Correspondence School offers distance education programs at the request of a school. These programs were once free but are now charged to the school. The programs include individual ESOL programs for students throughout the country whose needs cannot be met by their local school. These needs might include teaching L1 literacy to newly arrived adolescents or preparing students for employment in a particular vocation.

The Local Context

McAuley High School in Otahuhu, South Auckland, is located just one kilometer from the Southern Motorway, the highway that links Auckland, New Zealand's largest city, with the rest of the country. The district from which the school draws most of its students has a high population of Pacific Island families, many of whom are long-time residents. Churches are an important part of local life, representing all the mainstream denominations, some of which divide into separate congregations to accommodate different language groups. Local radio stations broadcast programs in the many languages spoken by immigrants in Auckland. The following account characterizes the diverse profiles of McAauley students: "Most students live in five or six worlds. They live in the world of their family, the world of their culture; for many, the world of their church; the world of school" (Hill & Hawk, 1999, p. 32).

Many students apply to attend McAuley from areas located outside the immediate district. This is because their families value the school's reputation as a girls' school that encourages academic excellence and has a Christian base. As the school's *Prospectus* (McAuley High School, n.d.) makes clear, residents tend to judge a school by the appearance of its students. Walking to and from school, or traveling by bus, McAuley students are easily recognized by their school uniform. (Almost all New Zealand secondary schools require students to wear uniforms.)

The School

McAuley High School, whose spring 2000 enrollment was 625, is situated in Auckland, the largest population center in a country of roughly 3–4 million people. Although most students reside in the local area, a number must travel a considerable distance to attend the school. Founded in 1963 and originally staffed by the Sisters of Mercy, the school now has a lay principal and staff but retains an association with its founding Catholic order, whose values and traditions are important in the daily life of the school. As summarized in the mission statement in the school's *Prospectus* (McAuley High School, n.d.), "McAuley High School offers a quality Catholic Education which challenges students to strive for standards of personal excellence" (p. 2).

In the educational jargon of New Zealand, the school is described officially as a Catholic Integrated School. In New Zealand, some parochial and all other private schools are designated as integrated, meaning they are allowed to retain their special character. McAuley, with its chapel literally and figuratively at the center of the school, is one of these. As part of its Catholic base, the school attends to all aspects of its students' development: spiritual, intellectual, emotional, and physical. According to the school's *Prospectus*, the Religious Education Program combines the Christian message with opportunities to experience Christianity in action through the sacraments, retreats, prayer groups, Amnesty International, and St. Vincent de Paul groups. The chaplain, who is a religious (i.e., a lay or ordained member of a celibate Catholic order or society) and a member of the school's teaching staff, arranges liturgies around special occasions, to which the student population contributes.

One of the school's aims is to help students "reach personal standards of excellence in academic achievement" (McAuley High School, n.d., p. 2). To this end, deans play an important pastoral and administrative role at each academic level. As a sign of the support the school offers, families unable to afford the school's (quite modest) tuition are encouraged to speak to the principal. The deans are responsible for seeing that students receive the help they need once they have been identified as requiring English language support.

The ESOL segment of the school population is not identified by separate labels, although for purposes of special Ministry of Education funding, statistics do have to be provided. The school population includes students from all of the categories described by the ministry: refugees and free immigrants, long-term settlers, and new arrivals. In addition, the population represents a range of ethnic groups. However, some groups are more dominant than others, as the following statistics show. Of the 619 students enrolled in 1999, the ethnic composition was as follows:

- 80.1% from the Pacific Islands, the two largest groups being Samoan (56.5%) and Tongan (17.1%)
- 8.7% European

- 6.5% Maori (the indigenous people of New Zealand, nearly all of whom speak English as their L1 and are therefore never included in ESOL statistics)

- 2.6% Asian

- 2.1% Other (African and Arab) (L. McQuade, personal communication, March 1, 1999)

Of these students, 433 were born in New Zealand but use the language of their parents in varying degrees at home and in their community. Their English language use was the focus of a recent informal, unpublished investigation by one teacher. Apart from these 433 New Zealand-born students, 81 others have lived in the country for 11–16 years. Even the 41 who have lived here for 6–10 years have had a large part of their schooling in English. Although only a portion of the 64 students (10.35%) who have been here for 5 years or less are eligible for Ministry of Education funding, clearly many more need some form of English language support.

Parents participate in school life in a number of ways, the two most formal being membership on the Board of Trustees and in the Parent-Teacher-and-Friends Association. As is the case in all New Zealand schools, McAuley is managed by a Board of Trustees, which consists of 5 parents, 1 staff representative, 1 student representative, the principal, and 4 members appointed by the bishop. This board governs the school and sets policy; the Parent-Teacher-and-Friends Association organizes functions throughout the year.

As a Decile 1 school, McAuley was selected to take part in two programs aimed at raising students' learning outcomes: Achievement In Multicultural High Schools (AIMHI) and Assessment for Better Learning (ABeL). These programs are explained in the Distinguishing Features section.

❖ DESCRIPTION

The general school program is based on the *New Zealand Curriculum Framework* (Ministry of Education, 1993), established in 1993 and detailed since then through specific documents in each curriculum area. The curriculum areas include language and languages, mathematics, science, technology, social sciences, the arts, and health and physical well-being. Students take the full range of these subjects, as well as religious education, and work toward the qualifying examinations, as outlined in Table 1.

Students' Options

ESOL students have several options for developing their level of English language proficiency needed for their curriculum studies. ESOL programs are organized in a progression that parallels mainstream courses and enables ESOL students to be mainstreamed as soon as possible. Table 1 illustrates these options.

The New Zealand School Certificate examination, which is the first of the national examinations, and the National University Bursary examination are conducted nationally and are the traditional track for students seeking academic qualifications to pursue tertiary education. In addition, the New Zealand Qualifications Authority (NZQA) approves smaller units of assessment called *unit standards*,

TABLE 1. PROGRAM OPTIONS FOR ESOL HIGH SCHOOL STUDENTS

Year	Mainstream Program	Additional ESOL Support
9	• curriculum classes in language and languages, mathematics, science, technology, social sciences, the arts, health and physical well-being, and religious education	• integrated studies class • out-of-class, small-group work • explicit, short-term language instruction
10	• New Zealand School Certificate examination (taken by some students in Year 10)	• Double English in addition to mainstream classes
11	• New Zealand School Certificate examination (taken by most students in Year 11) • New Zealand Qualifications Authority (NZQA) unit standards	• Double English (Students taking the New Zealand School Certificate examination take one less mainstream subject to allow them more time to prepare for the exam.)
12	• NZQA unit standards courses • internally assessed certificate • external examination (optional) (assessed nationally)	• Communications Skills English (a unit standards course with a practical rather than a literary orientation)
13	• National University Bursary examination • NZQA unit standards courses	• National University Bursary examination • unit standards courses

which measure students against specific criteria to meet a particular standard. Many of these units are in nontraditional subject areas that may assist students seeking employment in a particular vocational area.

The programs in each of the five secondary education years are described in further detail below. It is important to note that ESOL students may arrive at any time during the school year and at any academic level of the school. Although it is acknowledged that some students may need to spend time in a special English language program, the school's policy is to integrate them into the mainstream as soon as possible.

Year 9

As outlined in Table 1 and described below, there are three kinds of assistance available to students during their 1st year of high school.

1. Students in their 9th year may take an integrated studies class in which they study three subjects with the same teacher. The teacher of this class, a registered mainstream teacher, has had ESOL training and several years' experience with students from a variety of non-English-speaking backgrounds. Spending a large part of their week with the same teacher gives these students confidence and reduces the stress of their having to relate to the many different teaching styles found in the average high school.

This class is smaller than the average mainstream class and thus has a more favorable teacher-student ratio. Although some of the students who take this class are native New Zealanders, for a variety of reasons they need extra English language support for academic purposes. Others who enroll are recent arrivals to the country.

2. Students may meet in small groups outside the mainstream classroom for several hours a week to work on language skills and vocabulary, under the supervision of an ESOL teacher. The small-group work complements and reinforces the students' mainstream instruction by providing a less threatening forum in which they may ask questions and complete tasks set by the mainstream teacher.

3. Students may receive short-term, explicit English language instruction from an ESOL teacher in a separate room outside the mainstream classroom to facilitate their entry into the mainstream. Even these students, however, are quickly integrated into classes teaching more practical subjects, where they are teamed, if possible, with a student from the same language background. An ESOL support teacher will often assist these students and their teacher in the mainstream subject classroom.

Students in all three of the above groups may be supported in their mainstream subject classrooms by an ESOL teacher. Decisions about which types of assistance suit which students are made on the basis of a diagnostic entrance test and information from their previous schools.

Years 10 and 11

In the 2nd and 3rd years of high school, students may take a class known as Double English, which substitutes for one other course each day of the week. This class follows the mainstream English-language curriculum but devotes twice as much time to English-language instruction as other classes. For the rest of their academic requirements, students taking Double English are integrated into regular mainstream classes, where they may also be supported by an ESOL teacher. During Double English, students may be given time and support to work on tasks assigned in their mainstream classes. The following are extracts from the report of a Double English teacher.

> I have a Year 10 English/ESOL class. These 20 girls were identified in Year 9 as having low level competence in English according to a national language competency test. They are mostly second phase and all have been in NZ more than 5 years—mostly born here. The problems of all but two appear to be consistent with second phase language acquisition.
>
> The program they are following is a parallel of the requirements of mainstream English for Year 10. The main thrust of assisting these students is to give them "double" English—i.e., two lessons per day rather than one. The program is integrated rather than two separate programs—the second lesson each day serves to consolidate what was taught or done in the first lesson. These students respond to tight structure and variety but cope only minimally with normal paced delivery and only on familiar tasks. They work better in groups.
>
> There are several units of work which I have devised and followed based

on the broad guidelines for what has to be covered in Year 10, viz. library skills (research skills, information literacy, electronic accessing of data, etc.); literature—prose, poetry, and drama; visual literacy—static images, film-making, etc.; media and debating. Integrated into these units are the on-going wider reading (silent sustained reading, guided reading, and reading strate-gies—reading being a special weakness of the class); expressive writing in the form of an on-going journal; and grammar, punctuation, and vocabulary correction and enrichment. In addition, there is an ongoing emphasis on record keeping, note taking, organization of material, etc.

Years 12 and 13

In the last 2 years of secondary school, students receive ESOL support on a needs basis. For example, students may be withdrawn from the Communications Skills class to receive assistance with essay writing, or an ESOL teacher may attend main-stream classes with students to help them with subject-specific tasks. Two common difficulties ESOL students face are understanding the language of assignment questions and understanding the language of examination instructions.

In addition to traditional curriculum subjects taught throughout the country, ESOL students have the opportunity to study either Maori or Samoan during their 4th and 5th years of secondary education.

The Roles of Teachers

McAuley offers in-service courses that inform teachers about links between language and content learning. Two full-time ESOL teachers provide additional support. These ESOL teachers are mainly responsible for

- conducting initial assessment of students

- assisting in selecting students for ESOL classes

- assisting in the application of ESOL funding

- liaising with other teachers employed as a result of funding received

- maintaining records on students (assistance and progress)

- writing programs and learning outcomes

- liaising with the correspondence school

- purchasing resources

As noted above, some students receive additional ESOL support. Teachers are encouraged to identify special strengths of ESOL students, as illustrated by the following teacher's report about her Year 10 ESOL class.

> A pleasant surprise this week! These students are marvelous at debating style. When asked to express opinions in other formats, they are very hesitant—especially in writing or giving a talk on a subject. I thought them incapable of opinions. The format of the debate seems to be something very familiar and they are very comfortable with it. They really star in this and do it far better than native speaker students of their age. And amazingly, the quality of their ideas is rather high—never seen in an essay, or expressive writing on set topics, etc. Obviously, they favor some channels over others. It must be cultural!

In-class support by the mainstream or a second teacher is an important part of the mainstreaming policy in many schools, as stated in one school's policy statement reference to "organization of across-curriculum, in class support" (Kennedy & Dewar, 1997, p. 67).

Mainstreaming Principles

For the mainstreaming program to work, teachers of all classes have to be teachers of language as well as content. The five principles established in staff development programs that guide this approach are described below.

1. The subject content should be made clear by
   - building on students' out-of-school experiences
   - providing visual support

Content draws on students' firsthand experiences. For example, in a geography unit on work processes, such as farming, students compare food growing and production practices in their home countries. Pacific Island students are familiar with the growing, harvesting, and processing of coconuts, including how to use the husks and milk. This experience becomes the basis for talking about new farming processes, such as milk production in New Zealand. A field trip to a dairy farm helps to make clear the differences as well as the similarities in the different processes.

2. The language should be introduced gradually.

The technical terms of the subject and abstract terms commonly used in the language of study (e.g., *aspects, conditions, features*) are practiced until they become part of the students' active vocabulary. Traditional language class activities provide opportunities for students to use this new language, orally and then in writing:

- barrier games
- picture dictations
- sequencing
- cloze activities

3. Lessons should cater to a range of language levels.

Texts are available at different levels on the same topics. Tasks are graded to include students whose English is limited as well as those whose language skills need extending. Thus, in a follow-up lesson to a field trip, one group is asked to match photographs and labels while another is asked to plan a written report of the visit.

4. Lessons should cater to a range of learning styles.

Teaching and learning in groups rather than in the traditional teacher-up-front style builds on Pacific Island students' enjoyment of cooperative learning. It also makes use of the different learning experiences that students bring to the class.

5. Encourage students to use their L1.

Students can use their L1 at each stage: discussion, writing, and, where suitable resources are available, reading more on the topic. For example, in a lesson on the process of food production in the Pacific Islands, recent arrivals would be encouraged to discuss the steps in their own language. They might create bilingual posters to accompany written reports in English. Bilingual teachers on the regular school staff can provide a rich resource for reference. If experts in the local community are available, they can also be invited to share their knowledge.

◈ DISTINGUISHING FEATURES

The school's distinguishing features include special initiatives set in place by the Ministry of Education, ongoing staff development, and a mentoring system.

Ministry of Education Support

As noted earlier, support from the Ministry of Education comes through regular funding and special programs initiated nationally to improve the achievement levels of students in Decile 1 schools throughout the country. One of these is the AIMHI project, which is based in nine schools throughout the country and includes regular assessment as a way of teaching students how to learn. The principal of a neighboring school involved in the AIMHI program (in which McAuley is also taking part) reported that many parents were reticent about becoming involved in their children's academic achievement and school activities. The ability of parents to use their own languages in discussions made a positive difference (Rowe, 1999).

At the heart of the AIMHI program is the ABeL program. Although there are logistical hurdles in administering this program (e.g., it is time-consuming, and other students have to be occupied while teachers spend individual time with each student), teachers are persisting, according to the Rowe (1999) report, because they believe in the aim of student accountability.

> Teachers start with an objective for what they want to teach, then work backwards to plan the lesson. Clear criteria are set out so students know what they need to complete in order to achieve the high, but attainable standards. Students self-review using the criteria and take samples of work home to share with their families. (p. 16)

The time-consuming part is the conferencing, which involves individual feedback, including setting tasks, clarifying the process, and completing associated paperwork. However, teachers find that the time spent is invaluable because the information they gain helps them plan future units of work, and the students gain a better understanding of what is expected of them.

Staff Development

Another interesting feature of this school is its support of teachers' professional development. During the past few years, two teachers have been awarded full-time, paid university study leave to take courses relating to work with L2 learners who are mainstreamed: One teacher completed an MA in language teaching and wrote a thesis on the use of English by the school's Samoan students; the other, a science teacher, completed a diploma in English language teaching in 1 year and wrote a dissertation on tasks to link language and content development in the science area. In addition to these two teachers, who were released for full-time study, others have gained TESOL qualifications on their own time.

Another feature is the school's determination that each staff member should be seen as a teacher of English. To this end, staff have completed an in-service training program known as Learning Through Language, in which participants are made aware of the basic principles of language learning and teaching in relation to language demands in the various curriculum areas.

In the school's academic program, maintenance of students' L1 is strongly emphasized. In fact, one staff member is part of a team that is developing a national Samoan curriculum for high schools. Interestingly, a number of parents remain to be convinced that allowing their children to study their heritage language at school is a wise use of study time, even though the language has been taught for some time as part of the BA program at the University of Auckland. It is hoped that having had the Samoan language as an examination subject at the national level in high schools for the first time in 1999 will strengthen parental support for this program. New Zealand needs people trained bilingually, and tertiary-level courses in interpreting and translating are available to students who are coordinate bilinguals (strong in two languages). Career opportunities are then available to them in government departments.

Mentoring

A mentoring program is also in place. Former students who are now studying at the tertiary level (i.e., college and university level) are encouraged to return to McAuley to serve as formal and informal mentors. As an example, students who graduated the previous year return at the end of the first semester to talk to current senior-year students about what they themselves might have done differently to prepare for tertiary studies. Throughout the year after their own graduation, mentors offer subject-specific tutorials to seniors and mainstreamed students in the junior class. These tutorials take place in the regular classrooms, and although they are voluntary, attendance is high. Tutorials include direct instructional as well as question-and-answer segments. In addition, toward the end of the year when students are gearing up for the outside examination, mentors help students practice and analyze sample examination questions. There are also plenty of opportunities for students to talk informally with mentors about problems they are presently encountering and their future plans.

One advantage of using former students from the same ethnic groups as mentors is that they have experienced many of the same difficulties as well as challenges posed by parental expectations. Another advantage is that, being of a similar age, they can relate well to high school students, who can ask them questions they would be uncomfortable asking a teacher and discuss problems in their L1.

❖ PRACTICAL IDEAS

A number of practical ideas emerge in this account that can be adapted by schools elsewhere.

- Be alert to national and state initiatives that can be implemented at the local level.
- Offer professional development activities that will lead staff to take full responsibility for students' language development.

- Identify ESOL-related areas for research and encourage staff members to engage in this research.

Further practical ideas come from researchers in the AIMHI program (Hill & Hawk, 1999), who interviewed staff, members of the boards of trustees, students, and extended families from a number of schools. The researchers suggest that teachers

- telephone parents prior to report evenings and other important events
- use the local radio station to inform families about school and broader educational events (e.g., Pacific Island Radio offers entertainment and information about local events in several different languages)
- schedule flexible meeting times with parents to accommodate their various schedules
- involve community members, such as clergy, in liaising with families
- use enrollment time to inform and gather information from families
- explain to students why certain information is being sent home with them
- use the postal system for sending home newsletters and important documents, rather than relying on students to deliver the documents to their parents

◈ CONCLUSION

A recent study of provisions for ESOL students in New Zealand schools (Kennedy & Dewar, 1997) lists a number of characteristics of good programs for students of non-English-speaking backgrounds. These characteristics provide a useful summary of the points made in this case study about mainstreaming ESOL students.

First, a program should provide support for teachers within the school. At McAuley, ESOL teachers are supported through ongoing professional development programs, such as in-service training in the Language Through Learning program, and the parents' group. Visitors also comment on the collegial atmosphere among the principal and teachers. Staff are also granted leave time to obtain professional credentials, such as diplomas and MAs in English language teaching.

Second, the calibre and commitment of teachers determine the quality of a school's program. At McAuley, all teachers share the responsibility for developing language proficiency in new speakers of English. Because staff are recruited for their commitment to the school's ethos, the realization of this ideal is ongoing.

A third feature of a successful school is in-class support for mainstream teachers. At McAuley, the ESOL teacher spends some of her time working in regular classrooms so that the course's principal teacher is able to spread his or her time evenly among all students.

A further feature of a school with a successful ESOL program is that families and the wider community are involved in supporting and being supported by the school. McAuley parents are members of the Board of Trustees and the Parent-Teacher-and-Friends Association, which affords them a say in the school's management. Support for families is provided financially and in other ways. For example, school fees can be waived in cases of need, and parents are welcome to discuss other matters with the school staff.

Finally, support from outside organizations is important. As mentioned, the AIMHI program receives ongoing government support.

◈ CONTRIBUTORS

Denise McKay, who completed an MA in language teaching at the University of Auckland, in New Zealand, taught at McAuley High School in Auckland for several years.

Marilyn Lewis is senior lecturer at the Institute for Language Teaching and Learning at the University of Auckland, in New Zealand.

CHAPTER 4

It Takes a Class to Teach a Child: The Challenge Program

Kathleen W. Osgood

◈ INTRODUCTION

It sounds like a nightmare. You find yourself lost in a strange building one day, surrounded by hundreds of people milling about, speaking a language you do not understand. Finally, someone smiles at you, says something, and hands you a sheet of paper covered with odd characters. He points, pats you on the back, and leaves you on your own. You recognize the numbers on the paper and try to match them with the numbers on the classroom doors. In a fog, you enter a room. More noise. A gentleman turns to you and says something that sounds like a question, but you have no idea what he has said. You sort of shrug. He hands you a book filled with incomprehensible writing, points to a desk, then turns away. You seem to become invisible and remain so the rest of the day, without understanding or communicating, just feeling isolated; a true nightmare.

Unfortunately, this nightmare, with slight variations, occurs time after time in the lives of beginning-level ESL students. This is the immersion method of teaching a second language. Immersion is actually a very fast, effective way to teach a second language. Certainly the motivation for learning a new language this way is exceptionally high. It is, however, stressful and often upsetting to the ESL learner.

In past years I have discovered, much to my dismay, that most beginning-level ESL students go through the entire year with little, and sometimes no, positive interaction with their U.S. classmates. Positive interaction with classmates accelerates English language acquisition partly because it reduces stress. Interaction is essential to ESL students' sense of well-being. When they feel more at ease with their classmates, they are more likely to attempt speaking in class, showing their personalities, and giving classmates an opportunity to get to know them. Positive interaction heightens a feeling of acceptance and lessens fears of failure. Interaction, however, is seldom initiated by beginning-level ESL students, and their silence often makes them appear aloof and uninterested to their U.S. counterparts.

In response to this daunting set of circumstances facing new ESL learners, I sought to develop a program that could help them feel more at ease in the everyday classroom, thereby affording them an opportunity for greater learning. To this end, I now employ the Challenge Program, which I developed for beginning-level ESL students in Grades 4–8.

◈ CONTEXT

Our school district in Delaware County, Pennsylvania, in the United States, has relatively few ESL students, so I begin each school year anticipating whether any of last year's ESL students will return and whether there will be any new ESL students entering the school. Will I encounter any true beginners, those with little or no knowledge of English beyond *hi* and *okay*?

Teachers receiving new, beginning-level ESL students in their classrooms frequently contact me within the first week of school, sometimes within the first hour. Regardless of the time of year, I attempt to initiate the Challenge Program as soon as I learn of a new student's arrival. I use the word *attempt* because this initiative requires not only my efforts and willingness, but the regular classroom teacher's and the students' as well. Although the program has met with varying degrees of success, it has never been turned down by a classroom teacher.

◈ DESCRIPTION

Soon after an ESL student arrives, I meet with the classroom teacher or middle school team of teachers, depending on the school context, who will be working with the student. I have found that obtaining the approval and active support of these teachers from the start is critical.

In a team context, students rotate between four core subject teachers (math, language arts, science, and social studies). The team teachers have weekly meetings during which they discuss problems, solutions, and questions about the students. I attend one of these meetings to introduce the Challenge Program. At this first meeting, I explain that the purpose of the program is to foster as much positive interaction between the new student and his or her U.S. counterparts as possible.

When dealing with a team, I try to elicit help from one or two of the teachers because each classroom has a different mixture of students. The time and effort required of the classroom teachers should be kept to a minimum, but their commitment to the program and to the ESL student makes a significant difference. If the teacher presents a positive and enthusiastic attitude toward making the new student feel welcome, the other students tend to mirror the teacher's behavior.

In the early grades, K–3, native-English-speaking (NS) students see little difference between themselves and an ESL student. They communicate with relative ease. They demonstrate, use body language, and actually take over more difficult tasks on behalf of the new student. They quickly learn that the ESL student is good at some things and not at others; in other words, the ESL student is just like them. I find, however, that this interaction does not come easily or automatically beyond the second or third grade, due in large part to the dwindling amount of free time that elementary school students now have during the school day. Communicating with a beginning-level ESL student takes time. Therefore, I begin the Challenge Program at the fourth-grade level.

At the first meeting I have with a teacher, I schedule a time to visit his or her classroom a week or so before the arrival of the new student to talk briefly (10–15 minutes) to the other students. At this time I may give some background on the ESL program, but usually I get right to the main point, asking for the students' help teaching the new student English. I tell them about a shy ESL student I once knew who did not learn the names of her classmates until well into the spring quarter. At first she did not know how to say "What's your name?" Then she was too embarrassed to ask their names because of her accent, and, finally, she felt stupid asking them their names when she had been in class with them for months; she had missed her window of opportunity. To solicit the help of the NS students in welcoming the new student, I give them a series of challenges. The first challenge is to teach the new student their first names and, of course, to learn the new student's first and last name. I make it clear that none of the challenges will require the teacher to allot special classroom time. The students need to be creative and talk with the ESL student at lunch, recess, or during other free time.

Next, I tell the students I will return to verify that the first challenge has been met. I usually let the students suggest an amount of time they feel will be necessary to accomplish the challenge. They usually agree on 2–4 weeks per challenge. Scheduling brief return visits can be difficult, but they are essential to the success of this program.

Invariably the students ask me what will happen if they succeed in meeting the challenge (i.e., what is the pay off)? In addition to achieving a sense of accomplishment and camaraderie, I promise them a small treat (e.g., candy). Then, naturally, they ask what happens if they do not succeed? I assure them they most likely will. If they have difficulty completing a challenge for some reason, they have the option of extending the deadline or skipping that particular challenge and going on to the next one. I have found that requesting the classroom teacher to post a written notice of each challenge (supplied by me), complete with due date, is beneficial to students. It helps them remember which challenge they are working on.

◈ DISTINGUISHING FEATURES

The Challenge Program can be tailored to fit any class and implemented within a week or two of an ESL student's arrival. The first challenge, as described above, always focuses on getting acquainted. I may change the sequence of the other challenges, omit some, or add new ones, but I always start by asking the class to teach the new ESL student their first names as the first challenge. Knowing his or her classmates' names helps the new student to interact more comfortably and confidently. As an added benefit, all the students learn more about one another, such as who is outgoing, who gets embarrassed easily, who is shy, who is helpful, and so on. Although difficult to measure, the knowledge gained during this challenge is invaluable.

After this initial challenge, I sometimes design other challenges to coincide with classroom learning. For example, a fourth-grade class may be studying their home state. As a challenge, I ask the NS students to teach the ESL student the major physical features, cities, or products of the state. This activity aids classroom learning as well as English acquisition. Usually, however, I create challenges to complement everyday ESL work. For instance, lessons requiring memorization and repetition easily lend themselves to a challenge. Areas that need review are excellent for challenges. Sometimes I incorporate the information from a difficult lesson a class is working on into a challenge throughout the course of the year.

Another distinguishing feature of the Challenge Program is the simplicity with which it can address different age groups and interests. A vocabulary challenge, for example, will remain basically the same, but the words used as well as the number of words given can be selected to meet the needs of the ESL student and his or her class.

Occasionally, a class will complain that some students are not participating in the challenges. As a general rule, it is best to hold the entire class accountable for meeting the challenges. However, not every challenge will interest every student. When this occurs, I try to encourage those who did not get involved with one challenge to try with the next. I reiterate that this is a voluntary program, but that I hope everyone will help. Solidarity is desired but not essential for success.

The way I verify that a challenge has been met depends on the challenge. Sometimes I do this with the entire class; other times, I do this with the individual ESL student, depending on how confident I am that he or she will successfully complete the challenge, how supportive the classmates are, and how much time is available. Unless a map or spelling is involved, I verify most challenges orally, as with the first "Getting to Know One Another" challenge. If I choose to verify with the entire class, the students are immediately aware of their success or failure. If, on the other hand, I choose to verify a challenge outside the classroom with just the ESL student, the rest of the class must take my word that the challenge has been met. However success is measured, the results are viewed as a class effort, and the entire class receives the reward.

❖ PRACTICAL IDEAS

I have developed a number of challenges that can be adapted to fit a variety of contexts (see the Appendix). Although I have used all of the challenges listed at one time or another, I have not always used them in the particular order in which they appear (with the exception that I always start with Challenge 1), nor have I used the entire list with any one ESL student.

When discussing practical ideas, I cannot imagine a more flexible or immediately useful program. There are numerous logical extensions of this Challenge Program; an ESL parent or high school student could start a Korean Club or a club for Urdu, Chinese, Arabic, or any language. The school could inaugurate an International Day. A class could hold a Special Foods' Day, which might involve several classes or the entire school. The list of possibilities is endless.

It is certain, however, that asking NS classmates to participate in helping the new ESL student learn English fosters friendships and understanding. After working with ESL students (which is often a new experience for U.S. elementary school students), several NS students indicated a real interest in learning a foreign language themselves, usually the language spoken by the ESL student.

❖ CONCLUSION

The Challenge Program addresses the needs of beginning-level ESL students and, to a large extent, the desire of the other students in the classroom to get to know the new students. On an end-of-year written evaluation that I distributed to the students in one class, including the ESL student, I asked if the Challenge Program made it easier for them to talk to one another. More than 80% of the students said yes. Below are some of the comments the NS students made about the ESL student.

- "The Challenge gave me a reason to talk to him."
- "The Challenge made it easier to learn about him and for him to learn about me."
- "I found out he's a nice person and smart!"
- "The Challenge made it easier to get things going."

The results of one recent set of evaluations showed that 95% of the NS students had had a conversation with the ESL student and 65% said that getting to know him had given them more positive feelings toward people from foreign countries. These results tell me the Challenge Program has a positive impact. The ESL student becomes an integral part of the class with something to offer. Although it is the ESL student who must learn a new language and culture, in the end, all the students reap the reward.

With so many variables, the success of the Challenge Program will be measured differently each time. Trying to create the best challenge for the individual ESL student and the particular class keeps each effort fresh and interesting. Regardless, the Challenge Program will be successful in that the benefits to all the students involved will far outweigh any difficulties. Seeing the smile on the ESL student's face, seeing classmates' fingers crossed for good luck as the ESL student begins the challenge, hearing the spontaneous cheer from the class as the ESL student answers correctly, and hearing the applause upon completion of the challenge demonstrate a level of success that cannot be measured with a questionnaire. When the class helps teach the ESL beginner, everyone becomes a winner.

◈ CONTRIBUTOR

Kathleen W. Osgood received her degree in elementary education from Elmira College, in the United States. She has taught in New York and Pennsylvania, at the American School in the United Arab Emirates, and, for a short time, in Guadalajara, Mexico. Recently, she received the 2002 Untours Award for Excellence in International Education. She currently teaches ESL for the Rose Tree Media School District, in Media, Pennsylvania.

◈ APPENDIX: SAMPLE CHALLENGES AND CLASSROOM ANECDOTES

Challenge 1
Getting to Know One Another

Date Challenge Set: _____ Date Challenge Met: _____

Goal: (Name of ESL student) will be able to point to and say the first name of every student in the class.

As you point to each person in the class, including the teacher, ask the ESL student to say that person's name.

In one class I worked with, the ESL student was visibly nervous, her voice barely audible as she started saying the names of her classmates. "Jam-es," was pronounced as two syllables. As she progressed, her voice remained quiet, requiring me to ask her to repeat a few of the names. One student beamed when she said his name, exclaiming "I didn't think she'd remember my name." "I love the way she says my name," said another. The ESL student did not understand most of the comments, but she recognized the positive feelings of her classmates. Excitement built as she neared the end of the line. When she said the last name, the room erupted into spontaneous applause and cheers. She lowered her head and smiled.

Demonstrating successful completion of this challenge is, unfortunately, not always as dramatic as the account described above. Once a teacher requested that I not use class time, requiring me to work outside of class with the ESL student, using a class roster and photos of the students, which was not as satisfying an activity. The challenge, however, was met regardless of the method.

Challenge 2
Geography

Date Challenge Set: _____ Date Challenge Met: _____

Goal: When given a map of the United States, (Name of ESL student) will be able to locate:

> Pennsylvania
> Philadelphia
> Washington, D.C.

When given a map of the world, the other students will be able to locate:

> Taiwan
> Taipei
> China

Grumbles could be heard from several fourth graders. They did not know where "Tay-wan" was; China, maybe, but not that other place. "I know where Pennsylvania is. Can I help Susan?" Susan, the ESL student, needed no help.

This challenge takes the least amount of time of any that I have done. However, getting some students to participate has proven tricky; some will learn the geographic locations quickly; others will not bother to try. Some classes love this challenge; others hate it. When it works well, the class has a new outlook. They have a sense of the distance traveled by their new classmate.

Challenge 3
Clothing and Accessories

Date Challenge Set: _____ Date Challenge Met: _____

Goal: (Name of student) will quickly be able to correctly name and pronounce the 32 items in the packet when shown a picture of each item.

I prepare a set of pictures with the names of the items (e.g., jacket, not coat) written on the back of each picture.

Challenge 4
Food

Date Challenge Set: _____ Date Challenge Met: _____

Goal: When shown pictures of food items or the actual foods, (Name of student) will be able to say the name of the item.

apple	tomato	beans
orange	onion	potato
banana	carrot	pumpkin
cherry	celery	
strawberry	lettuce	
grapes	corn	
lemon	peas	
pear		

After the successful completion of the challenge, the students shouted "He did it!" "Yes!" "What's our reward this time? Same as last time?" Mysteriously, I promised them the reward would be something different. The ESL student and I then left the classroom to prepare the treat. We prepared a large bowl of fruit salad, consisting of most of the fruits named during the challenge. While cutting up the fruit, the ESL student again reviewed the names. Then he proudly carried the reward to his classmates. Fruit salad is always a favorite treat.

Challenge 5—Double Challenge
Holiday Symbols

Date Challenge Set: _____ Date Challenge Met: _____

Goal: When shown a holiday picture, (Name of student) will be able to identify and pronounce the holiday items pictured (e.g., for Halloween, a jack-o-lantern, a witch, a ghost).

Holiday Song

Goal: (Name of student) will be able to sing along with the class, saying most or all of the words correctly (e.g., Jingle Bells).

I recommend singing only one verse and refrain. I also supply a sheet with the words to the song.

If available in your school, you may want to solicit the help of a music teacher. You might also ask the ESL student to teach the class a holiday song from his native culture in his native language. This sharing can be a magical experience for everyone.

Challenge 6
George Washington and Abraham Lincoln

Date Challenge Set: _____ Date Challenge Met: _____

Goal: (Name of student) will be able to:

- spell the U.S. presidents' names
- tell what number president they were
- say the presidents' nicknames
- identify a picture of each president
- say when we celebrate Presidents' Day
- tell one interesting story or fact about each president (e.g., George Washington chopped down a cherry tree, was a general during the Revolutionary War; Abraham Lincoln read by firelight, became a lawyer, was president during the Civil War)

Although this activity may sound boring, I have had surprising success with it. Not only has it engaged the attention of NS students who suddenly discovered they had an interest in U.S. history, but it has allowed NS and ESL students to connect on the same level, as learners of the same content at the same time.

Challenge 7
U.S. Pledge of Allegiance

Date Challenge Set: _____ Date Challenge Met: _____

Goal: (Name of student) will be able to recite by him- or herself, as well as with the class, the U.S. Pledge of Allegiance. He/she must be able to recite it accurately (no more than two mistakes) and with correct pronunciation.

Because the ESL student is likely to hear the pledge every morning in school, I like to pose this challenge early in the year. However, some of the vocabulary may need to be explained to the ESL student in advance, which may preclude early use of this challenge. The age, maturity level, and native country of the ESL student helps determine the timing for this challenge.

Challenge 8
Poetry

Date Challenge Set: _____ Date Challenge Met: _____

Goal: (Name of student) will be able to recite a poem in Spanish and in English.

An enthusiastic language arts teacher in our sixth grade had taken Spanish in college but had had little opportunity to use it. A new student from El Salvador gave her a chance to shine. Her excitement about having a Spanish-speaking ESL student in her class was a tremendous boost to the student's self-confidence and a real spark for the entire class. The student felt welcome, valued, and encouraged. This particular challenge came from this teacher, who located a poem in Spanish so her ESL student could participate in the poetry unit. As with all teaching, the enthusiasm brought to the job is invaluable.

Challenge 9
Playing a Game

Date Challenge Set: _____ Date Challenge Met: _____

Goal: (Name of student) will learn the rules of how to play a new game. He/she will play this game with at least eight different people and will be able to teach this game to his/her ESL teacher.

For this challenge, I let the students pick a game that I bring to the classroom (e.g., Guess Who?, Sorry, Chutes and Ladders, Scrabble Jr.). The main skills I focus on include the students' ability to socialize, give directions, interpret directions, and ask questions.

This is a wonderful challenge to initiate during inclement weather, when the students are forced to have recess indoors. All students seem to enjoy the activity, even those who are normally reticent about participating in the challenges.

Challenge 10
Tongue Twister

Date Challenge Set: _____ Date Challenge Met: _____

Goal: (Name of student) will be able to

- recite the tongue twister written below, from memory, with no more than one or two mistakes

- know the meaning of the words *butter*, *batter*, and *bitter*

  Betty Botter bought a bit of butter, but she said, "This butter is bitter. If I put this bitter butter in my batter it will make my batter bitter. But a bit of better butter will make my bitter batter better."

Recitation of this tongue twister has met with much excitement: "Can I try?" "Ooooo, oooooo! I can do it!" "I helped him with it; ask me!"

Obviously, any tongue twister will do (e.g., Peter Piper; She sells seashells by the seashore). Betty Botter is one of the more challenging tongue twisters I have used because it contains many short vowel sounds that many beginning-level ESL students have difficulty pronouncing. It has stimulated some healthy competition, lots of laughter, and successful completion of the challenge.

CHAPTER 5

Breaking Out of the Billabong: Mainstreaming in Australian Schools

Sophie Arkoudis and Chris Davison

The meaning of change for the future does not simply involve implementing single innovations effectively. It means a radical change in the culture of schools and the conception of teaching as a profession. (Fullan, 1991, p. 142)

❖ INTRODUCTION

In Australia, mainstreaming was a concept first advocated by those seeking "to strengthen multiculturalism by bringing welfare, educational, and government servicing needs from the margins into the central concerns of core social institutions" (Castles, Kalantzis, & Cope, 1986, p. 2). It was part of a national move away from a focus on individual difference/deficit toward a reexamination of the nature of societal structures. Mainstreaming was quickly taken up by the ESL field as a way of pushing the whole school to take more responsibility for ESL learners, "reconceptualizing so-called 'mainstream' programs so that they cater adequately for the needs of the total population" (Campbell & McMeniman, 1985, p. 32).

The mainstreaming movement coincided with increasing concerns in the ESL field to align the content of ESL programs with mainstream curricula, partly to enhance the interest and relevance of ESL curricula, partly to ensure that learners continued their conceptual development while developing English language skills. This reflected the relatively early recognition in Australia that to wait for English language learning to be complete before assisting ESL students with learning and development in subject areas would be discriminatory, as subject area learning would be severely disrupted. In metaphorical terms, this can be seen as breaking out of the *billabong*, an Australian colloquialism for a branch of a river that comes to a dead end, and entering the "main" stream.

However, within the ESL field in Australia, mainstreaming is not perceived as a watering down of the ESL curriculum or as necessitating the replacement of ESL specialists. Rather, a mainstreamed ESL program is conceptualized as involving direct assistance—where an ESL teacher works with ESL students—and indirect ESL assistance—where the whole school is involved in teaching ESL students (Campbell & McMeniman, 1985).

Although it is widely acknowledged that mainstream teachers need "a stock of easily comprehensible strategies which will help them gain initial and then developing confidence in their ability to help their students become more proficient in English" (Herriman, 1991, p. 122), the ESL teacher is seen as a curriculum specialist, not simply a source of technical assistance.

In Victoria, in southeast Australia, the ESL profession has resisted any attempts to undermine the provision of ESL-specific services; at the same time, it has used the rhetoric of mainstreaming to argue for widespread changes in school policies, curriculum, structures, and attitudes. Considerable time and money have been expended to develop a common but inclusive mainstream curriculum and range of program options to suit different needs. It is a measure of the degree of cooperation between key stakeholders in ESL education that, to a large extent, these efforts have been successful. The way in which one school has taken up these choices in developing an integrated program for ESL students and some of the enabling conditions that distinguish this program are explored in the following sections.

◈ CONTEXT

Brunswick Secondary College is a large inner-suburban school in Melbourne, with a long tradition of enrolling a high percentage of students from culturally diverse backgrounds. It is one of the few government schools in Victoria that has a separate ESL faculty, thus acknowledging that ESL is a specialized field in its own right within the school. It also houses a semi-autonomous English language center for recent ESL arrivals.

At the time of this study, the school's student population was 643. Of these students, 95% were from a language background other than English. The largest group was Arabic speaking. There were also large numbers of students from Iraqi, Greek, Italian, Somali, Turkish, and Vietnamese backgrounds. Approximately 27% of all students from language backgrounds other than English received direct support from the college's ESL program. There are a total of 60 equivalent full-time teachers at the college, including 8 ESL teachers. Although demographic changes in the area have led to more middle-class enrollments, the school remains committed to its ESL population. As a result, the school is becoming even more skilled in delivering a common but differentiated curriculum for linguistically and culturally diverse learners.

The school also houses the Brunswick English Language Center, which provides intensive English language and transition courses for newly arrived immigrant and refugee students in the area. National ESL policy entitles all new arrivals to 6–12 months of English language study in preparation for entry into secondary schools. Thus, the educational background and ethnic composition of the center's population change as students enter and exit the new arrivals program throughout the year. At the time of the study, the English Language Center was serving 78 students, mainly from Chinese, Eritrean, Somali, Bosnian, Turkish, and Korean backgrounds, with support of one part-time and nine full-time ESL teachers. Approximately 60 students transfer from the center to Brunswick Secondary College each year. Multicultural Education Aides (MEAs)—speakers of Arabic, Greek, Chinese, Bosnian, Somali, and Vietnamese—also support programs in the college and the language center. There is a great deal of cross-fertilization of ideas between the language center and the college. They participate jointly in curriculum initiatives and pilot programs, and work together to provide newly arrived students with a smooth transition into the mainstream Victoria secondary school system.

One of the aims of Brunswick Secondary College is to enhance school retention rates in order to maximize opportunities for improving ESL students' English language skills. All teachers are expected to meet the language and learning needs of ESL students in their classes, regardless of the students' length of residence or language proficiency level. Thus, a major objective of the ESL program is to provide support for teachers through complex time-tabling, team teaching, and on-the-job, in-service training.

In developing appropriate curriculum goals, outcomes, and pedagogy, the school is guided by the Curriculum and Standards Framework (CSF) (Board of Studies, 1995, 1996, 2000a, 2000b), the common curriculum and assessment policy framework used in all Victoria schools. This framework organizes the curriculum into eight key learning areas, with ESL and English being conceptualized as distinct but closely interrelated fields of educational activity.

According to the CSF (Board of Studies, 2000b, p. 5), the broad goals of ESL programs are to help students develop

- a level of competence and confidence in using English that allows them, over time, to participate fully in social and school-based contexts
- conceptual and English language skills
- an understanding of the learning styles and expectations of the Australian school system

Such statements emphasize not only that the central concern of ESL teaching is English language development, through direct or indirect means, but also that ESL aims to enhance subject learning and induct ESL learners into the culture of the school as well as the broader Australian community. The document can be used in planning, implementing, and evaluating an integrated language and content curriculum, regardless of whether learners are in a mainstream multiethnic classrooms or separate ESL classes.

To implement such a curriculum, Brunswick Secondary School has provided a range of different program options and extensive support to all teachers. As a result, ESL programming at the school involves not one but many separate but interrelated decisions—decisions about curriculum focus, L1 input, modes of delivery, learner groupings, and teacher roles (see Figure 1).

ESL need, as determined by CSF outcomes, shapes curriculum focus. Curriculum focus varies in emphasis along a continuum from content (or subject matter) to language. However, even a curriculum focus at the language end of the continuum is strongly related to the requirements of the mainstream curriculum; in an ESL-in-the-mainstream policy context, such a relationship is perceived as essential and inevitable. Curriculum focus then shapes structural and organizational decisions, such as learner/teacher deployment and time-tabling options. This is a reversal of many common interpretations of mainstreaming, in which students are first mainstreamed, then teachers and programs are assumed to fall into place. In contrast, ESL policy in Victoria highlights choices in curriculum focus and program options, albeit choices that are always constrained and limited by the availability of resources. The details of the school program are provided below.

Underlying Principles: whole school planning and responsibility; policy, structural, and attitudinal support within multicultural framework; different choices to suit different needs at different times; focus on language development, not just language use

ESL need (e.g., as identified by ESL CSF)	High	Medium	Low
Curriculum focus	Language (integrated with content)	Language/Content	Content (integrated with language)
Role of L1			
L1 maintenance orientation (continuing systematic L1 development)	L1-medium content classes ESL with L1 support	L1-medium content classes L1 as LOTE ESL with L1 support	L1 and L2-medium content classes L1 as LOTE
L1 to L2 transitional orientation (L1 development until "coping" in L2)	L1-medium content classes ESL with L1 support	Some L1-medium content classes ESL with L1 support	L1 perspective
L2 support orientation (L1 used as incidental support for L2 learning)	L2-medium classes with L1 support	L2-medium classes with L1 support	L1 perspective
Time-tabling options	Intensive classes Similar-needs ESL classes with some mainstream classes (parallel and adjunct classes, electives, self-access, focused groupings, sheltered instruction)	Mainstream multiethnic classes with some similar-needs ESL classes (electives, self-access, focused groupings)	Mainstream multiethnic classes with flexible groupings Mainstream multiethnic classes

Student groupings	Similar ESL proficiency Age/grade level L1 background	Similar ESL proficiency Age/grade level L1 background L1/L2 groupings	Age/grade level L1/L2 groupings
Teacher roles*			
ESL teacher	Direct ESL teaching	Collaborative teaching/ direct ESL teaching Team teaching	Collaborative teaching Support teaching in content Resource for content area
Content teacher	Resource for ESL area	Collaborative teaching/ support teaching in ESL classes Team teaching	Collaborative teaching Direct content teaching

*Collaborative teaching is defined as a situation in which an ESL teacher and a content teacher cooperate in some way in the planning, implementing, and evaluating of a curriculum. Collaborative teaching may or may not include team and/or support teaching, although the reverse should always be true. Team teaching is defined as a mode of teaching in which the ESL and content teacher have "equal responsibility for all students in that program, and for the planning and teaching of that program. Teaching may occur separately but in a highly integrated way or it may be done jointly" (Ministry of Education, 1988, p. 16); ESL support teaching is defined as when "the ESL teacher assists the class or subject teachers" (Ministry of Education, 1988, p. 16) in mainstream multiethnic classes.

FIGURE 1. Mainstreaming: Programming Choices (Davison, 2001, pp. 32–33). Used with permission.

◈ DESCRIPTION

Within Brunswick Secondary College, the ESL program operates as an elective system across Years 7–12. ESL is timetabled parallel to English and shares the same broad curriculum content as mainstream English classes. In addition, ESL students also can be selected for ESL Math in Year 10 and ESL Studies of Society and Environment in Years 7–9. Careful consideration is given to the way in which the subjects are timetabled and set against other options in the overall school curriculum, so that ESL learners do not feel that they are missing out on classes. As a result, ESL students recognize the program as being a useful, integrated, and legitimate part of the curriculum.

Team teaching is also a key feature of the ESL program at Brunswick Secondary College. Team teaching is arranged after staffing for all the direct ESL classes has been completed. Priority for team teaching is given to classes at the senior level and upon the request of the mainstream teacher. During the study, most team teaching was in senior science classes. In team teaching, the ESL and subject teachers are present at every session and have equal but distinct responsibilities for the class.

Mainstream teachers draw on a great diversity of methods and approaches in their day-to-day teaching, which can be characterized generally as being ESL-aware and language-conscious (Derewianka & Hammond, 1991; Ferguson, 1991). In the ESL program, some quite elaborate and explicit teaching approaches that involve the specific integration of language, subject matter, and teaching procedures are used, most notably the *topic approach* (Cleland & Evans, 1984, 1985, 1988). This approach was developed by two Brunswick ESL teachers in the early 1980s to integrate the teaching of language and subject content. It is widely used in intensive language centers and ESL programs within Victoria as well as interstate. Elements have been adapted and incorporated into mainstream classroom practice, although not in any systematic way.

The topic approach consists of four key stages. In the first stage, the visual stage, the instructor uses a visual to present the conceptual content, and students use exploratory talk to develop their understanding. The instructor models terminology for students to practice. Students are encouraged to produce spoken and written sentences about the topic.

In the second stage, building a reading passage, students assess statements about the visual as true or false. Students then join, sequence, and organize the statements into paragraphs to form a tightly written piece that describes the topic as presented in the visual.

In the third stage, analyzing and extending a reading passage, students explicitly focus their attention on the language features of a reading passage through a variety of written exercises. Students may compare the first reading passage with a second, more complex passage.

In the final stage, creating a passage, students produce their own piece of writing, based on the informational and conceptual content of the topic, and hopefully using features of language encountered in the topic. This approach is used at Brunswick to develop integrated units of work of varying linguistic and conceptual complexity for the ESL program.

Students also have access to an after-hours homework club. The homework club is staffed by an experienced ESL teacher and operates twice a week. There is an

Ethnic Youth Officer employed at the college to assist ESL students in investigating alternative educational pathways. The college is also implementing a program called VPrac, which prepares ESL students for the demands of Years 11 and 12, the final years of schooling.

◈ DISTINGUISHING FEATURES

The program at Brunswick Secondary College is distinguished not only by innovative and effective grassroots integration of ESL and the content areas in terms of materials and methodology, but also by strong structural, curricular, and policy support from the educational system. These factors create an environment in which good practice can be institutionalized. This support has been built up through 20 years of sustained and extended collaboration between education authorities, professional associations, teacher educators, and community organizations. In Victoria, there is a systematic, integrated ESL and content curriculum—a clear pathway for ESL learners—that is linked to students' needs, qualified and accredited teachers, cross-curricular collaboration, clear teacher roles, and some L1 and cultural support. This policy and curricular support is what makes schools such as Brunswick effective. These distinguishing characteristics of the enabling school environment at Brunswick are briefly summarized below.

A Systematic, Integrated ESL and Content Curriculum

The ESL Companion to the English Curriculum and Standards Framework (Board of Studies, 2000b) is based on the assumption that there is a need "to control English language input, and systematically and explicitly teach English language skills to ESL students before the outcomes of the English CSF will be appropriate for them" (p. 1). It provides an overview of the broad overlapping stages of ESL development for the Years P-10 as well as "a benchmark of what might be expected of ESL learners given optimum learning conditions" (p. 2; see, also, Figure 2).

Each stage of ESL development is divided into three modes:

1. listening and speaking
2. reading
3. writing

Each mode is further subdivided into four strands:

1. communication
2. contextual understanding
3. linguistic structures and features
4. communication and learning strategies

The description of each stage consists of (a) a detailed statement of the curriculum focus appropriate to that stage and (b) a list of expected learning outcomes, expressed as action statements or competencies. Each outcome is accompanied by a series of performance indicators. The overall framework allows ESL students to select different pathways, depending on their level of schooling, level of English language proficiency, and L1 literacy or educational experiences. It also allows for variable

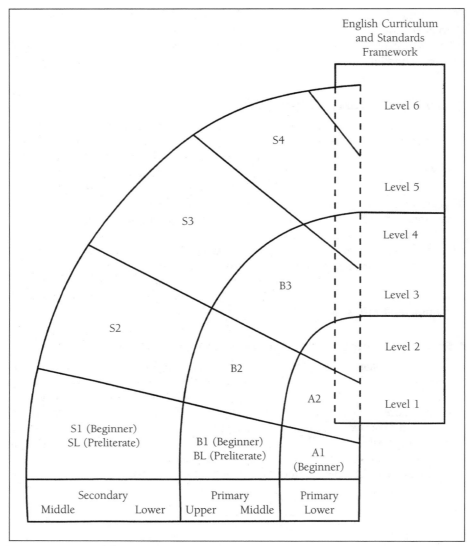

FIGURE 2. Stages of the ESL Companion in Relation to the *English Curriculum and Standards Framework* (Board of Studies, 2000b, p. 4). Reproduced with permission of the Victorian Curriculum and Assessment Authority, Melbourne, Australia. To view the full *Curriculum and Standards Framework II*, visit http://www.vcaa.vic.edu.au.

rates of development. The actual methods of assessment and choice of resources and teaching activities are left up to the teacher, although there is detailed course advice for different ESL teaching contexts (Board of Studies, 1997).

The CSF generally has been well received within the educational community, and ESL teachers, in particular, see it as critically important in affirming and legitimating their specialist knowledge and responsibilities. However, there remain a number of concerns about the CSF, including its reliability as a reporting tool and the reductionist and fragmented quality of its descriptions—an inevitable characteristic of standards-based curricula. One problem more specific to the ESL field is the way in which the framework maps onto the key learning area of English, thus suggesting that ESL is a subset of English and, therefore, that ESL learners move toward some unmarked cultural and linguistic norm. Within the ESL profession, many would prefer ESL to be conceptualized in curricular terms as a Language Other Than English (LOTE), as is Italian or Chinese, at the same time being integrated into and influencing all other key learning areas. There is ESL advice embedded within the course advice for each key learning area, but this is not seen as sufficient. On the other hand, the close relationship between English and ESL is obvious and desirable.

At Brunswick, the CSF gives coherence and purpose to mainstreaming. Upon enrollment in the English Language Center, ESL students complete an initial placement assessment, which the teachers have developed using the CSF. When students leave, the English Language Center provides a detailed report on each student. The syllabus is based on the CSF, covering at least one topic from each of the eight key learning areas, with content objectives integrated with English language learning. The college and the language center then assess the students according to CSF learning outcomes.

At Brunswick, the effect of the CSF on planning and teaching has been that the school has been forced to rewrite its curriculum within the CSF framework. The curriculum has become linked to triennial reviews and evaluation of programs in government schools. It has given ESL teachers at the language center and the college an opportunity to reflect on the work they have been doing and to write new curricula. It has also given teachers a common language with which to discuss ESL students' progress, especially as the students move from the language center to the college.

However, there have been several concerns raised about the impact of the CSF. One has been that ESL students' progress, in some cases, cannot be demonstrated based on the stages defined in *The ESL Companion to the English Curriculum Standards Framework* (Board of Studies, 2000b).

In addition, in the college, ESL collaboration has not always been sought by other subject departments in the initial stages of developing curriculum, with ESL issues belatedly raised at the lesson planning stage. Thus, the content curriculum, rather than the learners' stage of ESL acquisition, tends to dominate the language focus, making the whole process of developing integrated curriculum more time consuming.

A third problem is that subject teachers at senior levels are less willing to integrate ESL strategies and content into mainstream curriculum because they fear it will slow down the teaching of topics, thereby jeopardizing coverage of key content. However, attitudes appear to be changing as teachers become more accustomed to collaborating and making their objectives more explicit.

A Clear Pathway for Learners That is Linked to ESL Needs

The needs of ESL students, as described in and reported by *The ESL Companion to the English Curriculum and Standards Framework* (Board of Studies, 2000b) and its predecessors, are different at different stages of ESL development. Hence, different but integrated modes of delivery will be required at different stages of schooling.

Generally, older learners will require more direct ESL assistance than younger learners, but the language, literacy, sociocultural, and educational knowledge, attitudes, and experiences that ESL learners bring to the classroom may vary significantly, even when their goals and aspirations are the same (Aird & Lippmann, 1983; Campbell & McMeniman, 1985; McKay & Scarino, 1991). In terms of classroom and school organization, this conceptualization of an ESL program assumes an enormous variety of groupings and varying class sizes, depending on the needs of all students. It also implies a range of teaching arrangements, including bilingual teaching and cross-age tutoring as well as small-group conferences and team teaching.

It is assumed that almost all ESL learners will require regular and intensive small-group work with a qualified and experienced ESL specialist at some stage of their learning in order to gain access to the common curriculum and ensure the systematic development of their English language proficiency. This may be done through an introductory period in an intensive language center integrated into a school, timetabled parallel or elective classes, or flexible groupings within the mainstream classroom. However, the choice of the most appropriate delivery system for the curriculum is guided by the needs of individual learners, not by rigid ideology.

For example, at Brunswick, a recently arrived, preliterate, Somali refugee is not treated in the same way as a Greek immigrant who has studied EFL since primary school and has had successful and uninterrupted L1 literacy development and schooling before arrival. The latter may be able to build on his solid foundations in English and other content areas with ESL support in the mainstream multiethnic classroom, through individualized or parallel work, use of English-speaking background models, and judicious use of pair work, which extends participants in different ways. At Brunswick, such a student would also be likely to undertake 5 hours of common study English in a similar needs class rather than in a larger mainstream English class. By contrast, the Somali student will probably need a far more extensive period of adjustment to formal education and specialized instruction in ESL and literacy as well as intensive instruction in mainstream content areas, especially mathematics. It is far more effective in terms of student outcomes and resources to conduct such a program initially in a specialized but integrated environment, such as that offered by the English Language Center. Gradually, over a period of time, students in such a program would choose to transfer into a mainstream multi-ethnic classroom with ESL support, usually at different stages for different subject areas.

It is important to note that these kinds of flexible groupings are not defined as withdrawal. If you are not yet ready to enter a class, then you cannot be withdrawn from it. Rather, such students are seen as being enrolled in intensive, parallel, or similar needs classes, which are more appropriate to their particular needs. None of these arrangements is either compulsory or permanent. Thus, for example, in Victoria, you see quite a wide variation between regions and schools as to their preferred modes of ESL delivery, depending on their student profiles and resources. As you would anticipate, there is also more team teaching in primary than in secondary schools and more involvement in intensive language centers and schools by secondary than by primary students, due to differences in learning and teaching contexts.

This is not to suggest that all programming delivery issues in ESL have been resolved. It is worth drawing attention to a noticeable gap in program types in Victoria, an absence of maintenance, or even transitional, bilingual programs. In the mid-1980s, Brunswick, along with a number of other schools and language centers, was funded to operate a successful partial bilingual program, but when the additional funding dried up, so did the programs. There are some bilingual ESL programs in the primary sector, but none in the secondary sector. Bilingual approaches are limited to the incidental use of the L1 to support learning through English (the L2), and to the development of the L1 through separate LOTE programs. There are also public funding of MEAs, interpreting and translating services, multilingual materials and media, and after-hours ethnic schools. However, unlike the situation in the United States, the Australian ESL situation has been marked by rapid change in immigration and settlement patterns, with no single minority language group remaining or becoming dominant. This creates major resourcing problems, especially in the areas of teacher training and materials development.

Distinct but Complementary Teacher Roles and Responsibilities

This leads us to the question of the role and responsibilities of the ESL teacher in a mainstreamed ESL program. In Victoria, mainstreaming does not mean the end of specialist ESL teachers but, rather, a redefinition of their roles and responsibilities. This redefinition was first officially promulgated in *The Teaching of English as a Second Language (ESL): Guidelines for Primary and Post-Primary Schools* (Ministry of Education, 1987), which divides the ESL teacher's role into two separate but interrelated components—cross-curricular support and direct instruction—and establishes school responsibilities in relation to this role. The policy highlighted the vital role of specialist ESL teachers in relation to teaching, the assessment of student needs, and the provision of advice to other teachers within schools. At the whole school level as well as the classroom level, the ESL teacher is expected to be involved in and inform the planning, implementation, and evaluation of all key learning areas (Board of Studies, 1996; Ministry of Education, 1988). Such policy statements also have been critical in establishing an agreed-upon definition of ESL teachers and their qualifications and training.

With regard to the qualifications of ESL specialists, two National Conferences on TESOL in the early 1980s set groundbreaking recommendations for the field. In Victoria, these were reinforced by a State Conference on Teacher Education for ESL, Community Languages, and Bilingual Education (May 1985), the recommendations of which became policy for all the major ESL providers to children as well as adults. Influential state sector networks, such as the Joint Education Systems and Tertiary Institutions (JESTI) TESOL Forum in Victoria, maintain a watchdog role over the standards of TESOL teachers and facilitate productive dialogue between employers and teacher educators.

In Victoria, ESL teachers must have a specialist method as well as general teaching qualifications. An ESL method includes studies in language and language acquisition; TESOL methodology and curriculum design; policy and programming; the historical, institutional, political, and sociocultural context of Australian TESOL; and a minimum of 22 days of supervised TESOL teaching.

The Department of Education provides incentives to encourage teachers to obtain ESL qualifications, and there is an ongoing commitment to improve standards, although sometimes there are difficulties ensuring that policy is translated into practice. At Brunswick, however, all ESL teachers are ESL qualified, as are many mainstream teachers.

Practicing teachers also can access the publicly funded ESL in the Mainstream professional development program, which was developed in 1987 with Commonwealth funding and has been very successful in raising all teachers' awareness of ESL needs and strategies (Kay, 1991). The aims of the program (Education Department of South Australia, 1991, pp. 3–4) are

- to develop teacher's understandings of the language needs of (LOTE background) students and ways of meeting their needs

- to develop awareness of materials and teaching approaches that take into account the diverse cultural backgrounds and experiences of students in all classes

- to further develop the collaborative working relationships between classroom/subject teachers and ESL teachers in their schools

- to increase teachers' awareness of the need for ESL programs

This professional development offering is a 10-week course of 20–30 contact hours conducted by a teacher-tutor, with set reading requirements for each unit and between-unit activities. It is deliberately structured to ensure the commitment of the whole school to the in-service activity and the active participation of administrators as well as content or generalist classroom teachers.

In 1996, the whole staff at Brunswick participated in an ESL in the Mainstream course, which entailed 1 night a week for 10 weeks and much cross-curricular collaboration. In 1993, all staff participated in the Writing in the Science Area in-service course (Catholic Education Office, 1990), a cross-curriculum, genre-based course that focused on how to teach writing in different subject areas, which involved 1 night a week for 8 weeks. That the school actively promoted and participated in both programs indicates the administration's concern that mainstream teachers not only develop strategies for making subject matter learning accessible, but that all teachers take responsibility for language development.

However, there is some concern that the high profile and short-term gains achieved by such courses perhaps have obscured some significant limitations in their orientation and structure that are only now beginning to emerge (Arkoudis, 1995; Davison, 2001). Both programs emphasize pedagogy rather than curriculum content and need to be updated to take into account the influence and role of the CSF. Effective implementation also cannot happen without supportive administrative structures and policies at the school level and a positive, collaborative teaching and learning environment. Current Victoria ESL policy documents and guidelines advocate that an ESL teacher be on all the important decision-making bodies within the school and emphasize all teachers' shared responsibility for ESL students. It is not a coincidence that at Brunswick Secondary College a senior ESL teacher is the professional development coordinator for the school.

A Supportive Climate for Ongoing
Cross-Curricular Collaboration and Evaluation

Perhaps the most important distinguishing characteristic of the Victorian mainstreaming movement is the importance placed on ongoing cross-curricular collaboration and evaluation, demonstrated at the systemic level in the development of annotations to the Curriculum and Standards Course Advice and exemplified at schools like Brunswick by the official recognition given to ESL work in the school. This is demonstrated in exchanges, such as the following, between an ESL teacher, Victoria (V), and a science teacher, Alex (A), in a joint planning session around a genetics topic. In the transcripted dialogue that follows, the ESL teacher is attempting to explain the role of content in her teaching (Arkoudis, 2000, pp. 21–27).

V: . . . being your subject the content is apparent, whereas in mine . . . umm . . . ESL isn't a content in the same sort of sense and so it's more of the staging and the teaching and the learning process things that I would probably . . . in MY planning go about umm . . . and I think that's a problem sometimes with ESL teachers talking to subject teachers because we don't have umm . . . a sense of content in quite the same way, like we're a bit indiscriminate in a way, like to me almost it doesn't matter what the content, I mean it does matter. I don't mean that but I mean the . . . the content is a vehicle whereas for you the content is obviously more primary. Is that right?

A: Well [pause 3 secs] I find that a little bit difficult to accept in that . . . you know . . . I have a difficulty with the word CONTENT in what you're saying because REALLY content is something you must have an idea about otherwise you wouldn't really be able to structure anything . . . I don't think. Now you have to sort of ask yourself what you're trying to teach.

V: Yes. . . . I have linguistic aims and linguistic content you know but . . .

A: They sound really vapid but I know they're not.

V: (laughs) It doesn't matter whether . . . you know . . . that the . . . that the content that I'm dealing with is, you know, whatever topic in science or is in science or is in history or is in whatever . . . umm . . . I'm still enabled to teach the same linguistic structures and features and FUNCTIONS and umm you know . . . it's very easy to adapt to different . . .

A: But don't you start out if you do a lesson, don't you start out by saying OKAY today is, you don't say it's adverbs, you don't say today it's conjunctions. It's quite random which is covered?

V: No, no, no. It's not random at all umm . . . but . . . probably [pause 3 secs] you know . . . I'd think . . . you know . . . of what are the particular language functions so not . . . so not the structure so it's not adverbs and stuff like that. You wouldn't do that, BUT that you want students to be able to describe or to explain or to umm . . . justify or to you know THAT would be . . . that would probably be . . . you know probably come from more a functional we'd call it, in our terms we call it . . . in ESL terms we'd call it a more functional sort of approach and that we would be looking at different umm text types that they would need to use, to understand . . . to both understand and to produce, to be able to do that umm . . .

A: Can you see a place for that in what we are doing here?

V: Oh yes.

A: You can, because that's really interesting to me and that's the way we can find, I think, a way of working in this themed unit. In the work requirement that you've got there, they obviously have to write a report about this.

In the world of ESL, Victoria's description of her subject content needs no elaboration, but for cross-curricular collaboration to be a success, for the integrated language and content curriculum to be enacted, a common understanding of each subject's goals and assumptions must be reached. Victoria is experiencing, in B. Bernstein's (1996) terms, difficulty in recontextualizing her pedagogy to this cross-subject, disciplinary discussion. The science teacher, Alex, is having some difficulty conceptualizing a lesson without any content, particularly as he sees content as pivotal to his teaching. Victoria justifies how she plans lessons by using linguistic concepts that are not shared by Alex; therefore, he finds it hard to understand her perspective. Victoria is in a vulnerable position in this conversation because it foregrounds the science rather than the ESL curriculum, and Victoria lacks what Harrè and Van Langenhove (1999) refer to as the moral capacity to discuss science. Thus, at no point within this extract or the rest of the conversation does Victoria assert her opinion about the role of language in the science curriculum, in contrast to Alex, who is very forceful in his opinions about language teaching. Therefore, the ESL curriculum is positioned more as a methodology that offers strategies for teaching the mainstream content, rather than as a specialized content area with its own set of objectives for students that need to be integrated into and enhance the teaching of subject-area content.

This excerpt explicates the difficult and problematic nature of sharing pedagogic understandings across disciplinary boundaries, especially when those boundaries are still evolving. ESL teachers, unlike most of their mainstream colleagues, have embraced new forms of teaching, with only the vaguest of guidelines from curriculum developers and policy-makers as to the purpose and structure of such collaboration. However, the fact that at Brunswick such conversations not only occur but are, in fact, scheduled into the program appears critical for achieving success in implementing an effective mainstreamed program.

◈ PRACTICAL IDEAS

There are many things that can go wrong in mainstreamed ESL programs, particularly in collaborative teaching (Davison, 1992). However, in practical terms, the implications of this case study for developing a more effective mainstreamed ESL program are as follows:

- start with a strong sense of your own ESL curriculum and how it integrates with the content areas
- provide flexible pathways for learners
- negotiate complementary but distinct roles and responsibilities
- make the most of professional development opportunities to enhance your subject knowledge and your ways of working across the curriculum (and encourage your colleagues to do likewise)
- be positive but persistent in pursuing a clearer conceptualization of your common objectives and ways of working

◈ CONCLUSION

In summary, current Victoria policy includes broad agreement as to the definition of a mainstreamed ESL program, characterized by a distinctive but variable curriculum focus, flexible teacher and learner groupings and organizational models, and specialist ESL teachers. The definition is based upon strongly defined policies and practices in teacher accreditation and professional development for ESL and content-area teachers. Implementation at the school level is variable, but there are many schools, such as Brunswick Secondary College, that demonstrate that rhetoric can become reality.

◈ CONTRIBUTORS

Sophie Arkoudis is a lecturer in the Department of Language, Literacy and Arts Education, University of Melbourne, in Australia, and has had extensive experience working with secondary schools. She has researched and published a number of articles in the area of mainstream and ESL teachers' collaboration, and recently completed her PhD on cross-disciplinary pedagogic interaction and its implications for ESL practice.

Chris Davison is an associate professor in English Language Education at the University of Hong Kong, SAR, China, on extended leave from the Department of Language, Literacy and Arts Education, University of Melbourne, where she worked for many years in TESOL teacher education. She has published widely in the area of mainstreaming and ESL issues and has carried out extensive consultancy work on mainstreaming in schools in the Asian region. She is a former president of the Australian Council of TESOL Associations.

PART 2

Postsecondary Programs

CHAPTER 6

The Transitional Program: Involving Content-Area Faculty in Mainstreaming

Judith W. Rosenthal

◈ INTRODUCTION

Numerous studies have shown that undergraduate and graduate students who have successfully completed college- and university-level ESL programs often feel unprepared to take mainstream courses taught in English (Christison & Krahnke, 1986; Ostler, 1980; Sheorey, Mokhtari, & Livingston, 1995; Smoke, 1988; Valentine & Repath-Martos, 1997; for a review of this topic, see Rosenthal, 2000a). Whether it is the ability to take lecture notes, write papers, read textbooks, or participate in group discussions (just to name a few of the typical kinds of activities that take place in college classrooms), many students of limited English proficiency find it extraordinarily demanding to apply the knowledge and skills they have recently acquired in their ESL classes to the learning of new subject matter taught in English.

In addition, a number of studies reveal that mainstream faculty also have reservations about the academic preparedness as well as the language proficiency of ESL students enrolled in their courses (Ferris & Tagg, 1996; Horowitz, 1986; Johns, 1981; Powers, 1986; Santos, 1988; Vann, Lorenz, & Meyer, 1991; Vann, Meyer, & Lorenz, 1984).

At Kean University in the mid-1980s, faculty and administrators began expressing similar concerns about the difficulties some ESL students were encountering when exiting the ESL program and enrolling in mainstream courses taught in English. As a result, by the late 1980s, Kean established a new program to help address these issues (Rosenthal, 1992). This new program (originally called the Bridge Program, but shortly thereafter renamed the Transitional Program) focused on the kinds of support that faculty in all academic disciplines could provide to ESL students enrolling in their lower level, content-area, general education courses (e.g., introductory anthropology, biology, math, psychology, sociology).

◈ CONTEXT

Kean University, located in Union, New Jersey, in the United States, serves an extraordinarily diverse student population and enrolls more than 11,300 students (about 9,500 undergraduates and 1,800 graduate students). As a comprehensive teaching university, it offers 45 undergraduate and 21 graduate majors, granting, respectively, baccalaureate and master's degrees. In terms of Kean's student profile, about 58% of the students are listed as White (and non-Hispanic), 18% as Hispanic, 18% as African American, and 6% as of other ethnic backgrounds. Kean students are often the first in their families to attend college, and many are working and raising families while going to school.

The university directly addresses the linguistic needs of its nonnative-English-speaking (NNS) students through two programs: the Spanish Speaking Program and the ESL program. Among its many functions, the Spanish Speaking Program allows incoming students who are native Spanish speakers to begin their college studies by taking credit-bearing, introductory, general education courses taught in Spanish. These students, however, are concurrently enrolled in Kean's ESL program. As their English proficiency increases, the students decrease the number of Spanish-taught content-area courses that they take until they are completely mainstreamed. (Programs of this type are found at a number of colleges and universities across the United States and are described in Rosenthal, 2000b.)

Kean's ESL program serves about 500 students per semester. To participate in the ESL program, students must be matriculated at Kean and working toward a degree. After initial testing, they are placed in one of four ESL levels, and as they progress through the program, they can earn up to 15 credits toward graduation. (For a complete description of Kean's ESL program, see Reppy & Adames, 2000.) Although Kean's ESL student population represents more than 50 countries and speaks more than 40 languages, typically, at least 70% are native Spanish speakers. Nevertheless, as Reppy and Adames (2000) pointed out, "[I]t appears that, with some exceptions, whenever there is an economic or political upheaval somewhere in the world, it eventually is reflected in the ESL classroom" (p. 74). Thus, Kean's ESL program periodically receives influxes of students from various parts of the world experiencing turmoil (e.g., Vietnam, Russia, Haiti).

Kean's Transitional Program is open to students in the ESL and Spanish Speaking programs, and participation is completely voluntary. The Transitional Program allows NNS students who are particularly anxious about taking mainstream classes to enroll in introductory, general education courses assigned to content-area faculty who—by virtue of training they have received—can provide the kinds of academic and linguistic support ESL students may need.

◈ DESCRIPTION

In a typical fall or spring semester, the transitional sections (specially designated classes) regularly include such courses as Cultural Anthropology (3 credits), Principles of Biology (4 credits), Speech Communication (3 credits), Ceramics I (3 credits), Photography (3 credits), Introductory Algebra (no credit), Foundations of Mathematics (3 credits), Music Survey (3 credits), Introduction to Philosophy (3 credits), General Psychology (3 credits), Introduction to Sociology (3 credits), and several interdisciplinary, core, general education courses, such as Emergence of the Modern World (3 credits), Intellectual and Cultural Traditions of Western Civilization—1450 to the Present (3 credits), and Science and Technology in the Modern World (3 credits). Additional courses are offered on a less regular basis, depending on the availability of certain instructors to teach them as transitional sections. Although only 14 separate courses are listed above, some instructors teach multiple sections. Therefore, the program is able to offer a total of about 30 transitional sections per semester.

In each transitional section, a few places are reserved for students who register through the Transitional Program. The remaining places are open to all Kean students who meet the course prerequisites. Thus, the majority of students in a given transitional section are native-English-speaking (NS) and the remainder are NNS. Among the latter are those who have registered through the Transition program and perhaps a few more who, unwittingly, have selected a transitional section.

Transitional sections are taught solely in English and use the same text and follow the same syllabus as all the other sections of the same course. The instructors of the transitional sections are members of the various academic departments at Kean, and most are full-time resident faculty. Only a few are bilingual, although it is not necessary to be bilingual to teach in the Transitional Program. The majority of these instructors have voluntarily participated in a variety of relevant training activities, such as workshops conducted by ESL specialists brought in from other institutions as well as by members of Kean's ESL faculty. The workshops address topics such as the development of reading and writing skills by ESL students, linking content and language, and the mainstreaming process. Panels of ESL students have held lively discussions in front of faculty audiences about what works and what does not work well for them in the mainstream classroom. Instructors in the program also periodically receive copies of articles that address ESL topics, such as immigration trends, schooling issues related to immigrants, the second language acquisition process, and tips for teaching students of limited English proficiency. It is the Transitional Program coordinator who organizes and advertises the workshops (often in conjunction with the directors of Kean's ESL and General Education Programs) and who selects reading materials and distributes them to Transitional Program faculty.

Transitional Program instructors are encouraged to (a) reinforce the language skills the students acquired in their ESL classes; (b) foster interaction between students of limited English proficiency and their NS classmates; and (c) provide the type of linguistic support, modifications of teaching strategies, and classroom atmosphere that will facilitate the learning of subject matter by ESL students.

It is the instructors themselves who decide which modifications they are comfortable making to better accommodate the ESL students in their courses. Based on information they obtain from the training sessions and materials sent to them, the instructors may pick and choose what works best in their classrooms. Changes may be as small as writing key terms on the chalkboard or increasing the use of visual aids, or as big as providing written outlines for each lecture and being willing to spend considerable amounts of time with students as they write and revise reports and papers. Short and long lists of tips for teaching students of limited English proficiency are distributed to Transitional Program faculty on a regular basis, reminding them of what options they might wish to consider. Needless to say, not only do the ESL students benefit from these changes, but so do many of the underprepared NS students also enrolled in transitional sections. (Many of these teaching tips appear in other publications, such as Rosenthal, 1992, 1996, 1997.)

Students learn about the Transitional Program from their instructors and academic advisors in the ESL and Spanish Speaking Programs. Furthermore, the counselors for the Exceptional Educational Opportunities (EEO) Program, which also serves a number of ESL and Spanish-speaking students, inform their students about the Transitional Program. A campus flyer about the Transitional Program is distributed by the ESL, Spanish Speaking, and EEO programs and is also made available to the academic advisors in the offices of the school deans. The flyer—written in English and Spanish—provides information about the program, such as what it does, how students can participate, where to obtain additional information, and how to register for transitional sections.

During advanced and in-person registration, students seeking counsel from the three programs mentioned above can receive written permits to register for specific transitional sections. In addition to being NNS students, those who participate in the Transitional Program must do the following:

- successfully complete Writing in English I (a Level 3, pass/fail, high intermediate, prefreshman composition writing course offered through the ESL program that carries 6 credits toward graduation)

- meet the prerequisites for any transitional section in which they want to enroll (which are rare, however, because most transitional courses are at the freshman or 1000 level and do not have prerequisites)

After receiving advisement, students take their Transitional Program permits to the registrar's office, where they are guaranteed a seat in the designated course.

◈ DISTINGUISHING FEATURES

The principal distinguishing feature of the Transitional Program is that it is not part of Kean's ESL program and is therefore neither housed in nor run by the latter. It is a mainstreaming program, coordinated by a mainstream faculty member, involving mainstream content-area courses that are taught by mainstream faculty members.

The Transitional Program is also relatively inexpensive to operate, which has helped ensure its continuation to this date, more than 10 years after its initial funding (from an Ethnolinguistic Grant from the State of New Jersey) ran out. As the Transitional Program coordinator, I receive 3 hours of released time in the fall and spring semesters to plan the course offerings, organize registration, recruit and train faculty members, and manage other program-related administrative duties. My school's dean as well as the dean of the School of Liberal Arts and the director of Kean's General Education Program provide financial support for the program, such as paying for refreshments at workshops and printing the program's flyers and other materials. Staff members of the ESL, Spanish Speaking, and EEO programs all assist in advising students about the Transitional Program, and the registrar's office is most helpful in reserving places for students in the transitional sections. The director, staff, and faculty of the ESL program also offer support to the Transitional Program and faculty as needed. Thus, the continued existence of the Transitional Program depends on the goodwill and collaboration of various university offices, not on a big budget.

From the description provided so far, one might conclude that all is well with the Transitional Program. Undoubtedly, the heart and spirit of the program are in the right place, and it would be hard to imagine that the program is not benefiting the targeted student population. Unfortunately, we do not have the resources to collect the kinds of data needed to determine if the transitional sections, with their trained instructors, actually have a positive impact on the ESL students enrolled in them (based on criteria such as higher grades or a greater likelihood to remain in a specific course or in college), as compared to ESL students with matching profiles who enter the mainstream without participating in the Transitional Program.

There are other ongoing problems associated with the Transitional Program that we have been unable to resolve. One has to do with the registration and participation of students and the other with faculty recruitment.

Registration and Student Participation

Three aspects of registration and student participation are particularly troublesome. First, although 40–90 students may be issued permits to enroll in transitional sections in a typical semester, only half actually register and remain in those courses throughout the term. The other half either do not register or withdraw from the courses early in the semester. Needless to say, we would like to see a higher percentage of students in the Transitional Program enroll and remain in the transitional sections for which they were issued permits.

However, before jumping to the conclusion that this is a registration problem inherent only to the Transitional Program, we would need to examine enrollment patterns in other programs at Kean that also require not only written permission to register but also in-person registration. Unfortunately, most programs of this nature (e.g., Developmental Studies) are mandatory, whereas the Transitional Program is voluntary.

A second explanation for the decreased registration in the Transitional Program may be the somewhat recent elimination of in-person registration and the implementation of a streamlined telephone registration process (T-REG). This new system appears to have brought about a decrease in the number of students seeking advisement and, thus, a decrease in the number being issued permits for transitional sections. Quite simply, it may be that students simply wish to avoid any form of in-person registration whenever possible.

However, it is still too soon to reach a specific conclusion about the long-term impact of T-REG on enrollments in the Transitional Program. In fact, students may eventually find that in-person registration for a transitional section may be easier than before now that long registration lines have been eliminated.

The third registration concern is that many students who are eligible to participate in the Transitional Program choose not to, for reasons that are unknown. For example, in the fall of 1998, there were approximately 200 students enrolled in advanced ESL courses, for which successful completion of Writing in English I was a prerequisite. Although all of these students could have participated in the Transitional Program, few did. There are several possible explanations for this trend. For one, ESL students are not receiving adequate advisement; they do not feel as though they need the support of transitional courses, they cannot fit them into their schedules, or they believe the subjects are unnecessary. Another possible explanation is that ESL students take advice from other ESL students about which mainstream courses are less difficult and register for these courses instead.

Faculty Recruitment

The other particularly troublesome aspect of the Transitional Program is considerable reluctance on the part of most content-area faculty to participate. Program advertisements, campus-wide invitations to attend workshops, discussions with chairpersons asking for recommendations of faculty members in their departments who might be interested in teaching in the program, and personal phone calls have all elicited only a small positive response. In fact, there are only about 20 faculty members who regularly volunteer to teach transitional sections, and they are primarily from two of Kean's four schools (the School of Liberal Arts and the School of Natural Sciences, Nursing, and Mathematics). Attempts to involve faculty members from the School of Business, Government and Technology and the School of Education, have been relatively unsuccessful.

Persuading colleagues across the curriculum to consider the linguistic needs of ESL students who enroll in their courses is my most difficult job as coordinator of the Transitional Program. Based on discussions with them, I have concluded that there are essentially four explanations for their unwillingness to participate in the Transitional Program.

First, volunteering to participate in a program for which there is no financial remuneration or little recognition in terms of retention, tenure, and promotion does not have a great deal of appeal.

Second, many Kean faculty already feel that they are too busy to take on one more task. Besides their regular faculty responsibilities (e.g., teaching, grading papers and lab reports, keeping up with the newest developments in their academic disciplines, doing research, serving on committees, publishing, learning the latest computer technologies, advising students), they have been inundated by training and development workshops related to the most recent trends in higher education (e.g., multiculturalism, learning styles, writing across the curriculum, critical thinking, distance learning, service learning). They have been urged to incorporate what they have learned into the courses they currently teach, based on persuasive arguments about how such changes will make them better teachers, thus benefiting Kean's students. Unfortunately, the semester has not grown any longer, and finding time to integrate these newer concerns is difficult when there is already inadequate time to cover the existing course content in sufficient breadth or depth. In this context, the Transitional Program may seem like an added burden to faculty members who are already overwhelmed and fear that ESL students will take up too much of their time and energy.

Third, there exist many misconceptions about the nature of ESL instruction and ESL students. Unfortunately, college faculty are not immune to these, and many adhere to the belief that

- ESL is a form of remediation
- it is the sole responsibility of the English or ESL faculty to teach English
- students who successfully complete an ESL program will achieve reading, writing, speaking, and listening skills in English comparable to those of NS students
- it is possible for adult, college-age students to achieve near-native proficiency in English within the few short years they spend attending college

- ESL students who still have difficulty with one or more skill areas in English do not want to learn English, do not study, are not smart enough to be in college, and should not be taking mainstream courses

- ESL students who encounter difficulties in mainstream courses do not study, are not smart enough to be in such courses, are not smart enough to be in college, and should be sent back to the ESL program

- if you cannot speak English, you do not belong in college, and, in any case, knowledge can only be acquired by studying in English

Without a doubt, there are times when ESL students do not do well in mainstream courses because they are not academically prepared for college- or university-level course work, their English language skills are not yet up to the level needed to succeed, or, perhaps, they are not studying. However, the same can be said for some NS students. Thus, it is often difficult to pinpoint the precise reasons ESL students encounter difficulties in the mainstream classroom. It is much easier for mainstream faculty to blame the student (e.g., for not studying or for not trying hard enough) or the ESL program (e.g., for not adequately preparing the student) than it is to ask what they might do to facilitate learning on the part of the ESL student.

Fourth, people's attitudes toward immigrant L2 learners are often negative and inflexible to begin with, such that rational arguments based on research findings have little influence. In other words, it is of limited benefit to inform faculty about: (a) the increasing linguistic diversity of today's undergraduates, (b) the nature of the second language acquisition process, (c) the length of time needed to develop the level of L2 proficiency required to perform college-level course work, (d) the results of numerous studies that demonstrate that ESL students who have successfully completed their ESL programs often still feel unprepared and insecure about entering mainstream classes, and (e) that today's immigrants to the United States need considerably more formal education and highly refined skills than previous waves of immigrants if they are going to achieve their goals. Unskilled and uneducated workers, including those who are NS and NNS, cannot support their families and make ends meet if earning only the minimum wage.

It is ironic, however, that regardless of the reason for not wanting to participate in the Transitional Program, instructors from every academic discipline at Kean are teaching NNS students. This is a result of the diverse nature of the student population and the fact that all students eventually leave the ESL and Spanish Speaking programs and are mainstreamed, with or without support from the Transitional Program. Therefore, there is sufficient reason to argue that all instructors need some training in how to support the needs of ESL students who are studying their subjects.

Fortunately, in recent years, Kean's Center for Professional Development has begun a mandatory program to help acclimate first-year resident faculty to the academic needs of the university's particular student population. As a result, I have been asked, as coordinator of the Transitional Program, to facilitate a number of workshops in which a group of Kean's ESL students discuss those aspects of academic English that they find to be most troublesome as well as teaching behaviors that help or hinder their ability to learn in mainstream classrooms. The discussions are unrehearsed, uncensored, and informative. Faculty members in the audience have the opportunity to ask the students questions, and feedback from these workshops has been extremely positive. Faculty members invariably comment on how much they have learned from hearing directly from the ESL students, and the student participants are pleased to have had the opportunity to share their perspectives with a receptive group of faculty members.

My emphasis on the important role that mainstream faculty play in the success of ESL students does not in any way imply that college-level ESL programs are inadequate. At Kean, I have the most profound respect for my ESL colleagues and marvel at their ability to teach classrooms of students whose native languages include Haitian-Creole, Portuguese, Russian, Farsi, Mandarin, and Tagalog, and within a relatively short period of time prepare many of these NNS students to enroll in mainstream, postsecondary courses. The incredible academic success of Kean's ESL students reflects the excellence of our ESL program and the high levels of motivation and willingness of the faculty to work hard on behalf of the ESL students.

◈ PRACTICAL IDEAS

Unquestionably, any college or university that serves a sizable population of students of limited English proficiency could readily implement its own version of Kean's Transitional Program. I would encourage those attempting to do so to consider the following suggestions.

Gain Administrative Support

First, it is important to enlist the support of the administration to support the program, and gaining that support may require some persuasion. The academic needs of students of limited English proficiency may not be a top administrative priority. Moreover, administrators may adhere to some of the misconceptions previously described in this chapter. Nonetheless, most institutions of higher education are concerned about retention and graduation rates, and the value of a program such as the Transitional Program can be presented from that perspective.

Design the Program Carefully

Once administrative support is gained, a committee of interested faculty, staff, and members of the administration should begin meeting to design a program that best fits the needs of the ESL students and the institution. For instance, establish an ongoing process for coordinating faculty training, student recruitment, advisement, and registration. Organize a series of workshops to facilitate the training of mainstream faculty members. Decide where the program will be housed, who will run it, which students will be eligible to participate, and how registration will be handled. Determine how and where to advertise the program so that faculty and students are well informed of its existence.

Assuming that institutions have their own ESL programs, the resident ESL faculty—or, if funds are available, outside consultants and specialists—could provide appropriate training to content-area faculty. Such training will also help to identify content-area faculty on campus who are interested in the mainstreaming process as well as one or more individuals who might be willing to coordinate such a program.

Establish Evaluation Procedures

If an institution has the means to do so, it should develop an evaluation process to determine if the new program is actually having a favorable impact on the students it is serving. Appropriate data collection and analysis would be essential. As I mentioned previously, at Kean, this is one of the major weaknesses of our program. Although anecdotal feedback has been positive, we currently do not have the resources to evaluate the Transitional Program properly. However, this is not just the case with the Transitional Program, but is equally true of many academic support programs on our campus and at other institutions.

The difficulties in establishing a Transitional Program for mainstreaming ESL students have already been addressed in this chapter. Persuading the administration that the program is needed, recruiting and training faculty participants from across the curriculum, devising ways to advise and register students, and having the resources to evaluate the program on an ongoing basis are just some of the hurdles that will be encountered along the way. Nonetheless, once there is administrative backing, an institution can establish such a program. Certainly there are features of Kean's program that can be used at other colleges or universities, but modifications may very well be necessary to make the program a better fit for a particular institution.

❖ CONCLUSION

The Transitional Program is only one of a number of ways in which Kean University has attempted to address the mainstreaming needs of its ESL students. For example, like many other institutions (Kasper, 2000), Kean has incorporated content-based language instruction into its ESL curriculum (Reppy & Adames, 2000). Our ESL program also provides tutoring services to its students, as do many other support programs on our campus.

Kean's Transitional Program can easily serve as a model for other institutions grappling with ways to help in the mainstreaming of ESL students. Even with the problems described previously in this chapter, this low-budget program has the potential to help relatively large numbers of students and to increase retention rates.

At Kean, we are trying to educate content-area faculty about the important role they play not only in helping NNS students further develop their proficiency in English but also in contributing to the ultimate academic achievement of such students. The learning of English is not limited to an ESL classroom, and for some ESL students, the Transitional Program or a program like it may make all the difference between academic success and failure, remaining in college or dropping out.

❖ CONTRIBUTOR

Judith W. Rosenthal is the author of *Teaching Science to Language Minority Students* (Multilingual Matters, 1996) and the editor of *Handbook of Undergraduate Second Language Education* (Lawrence Erlbaum, 2000). She is a professor of biological sciences at Kean University, in Union, New Jersey, in the United States, where she teaches biology in English and Spanish.

CHAPTER 7

Cutting and Pasting Together a Successful Postsecondary Transition Program With Limited Budget and Staff

Thomas A. Upton

◈ INTRODUCTION

In the early 1990s, the University of Wisconsin-Eau Claire (UWEC) faced the ethical dilemma of admitting nonnative-English-speaking (NNS) immigrants and refugees who were academically at risk, while not being able to provide the academic and language support the students needed to be successful. This chapter provides a description of a 1-year transitional academic program, the Commanding English Program (CEP), designed to address the language and learning needs of these students as well as help them better integrate into the university community. CEP's success is reflected not only in noticeable student improvement but also in the collaboration of many university departments and units in the creation of an efficient and cost-effective administrative structure with limited institutional financial support.

◈ CONTEXT

The Setting

UWEC, a comprehensive university with 10,000, students, located in a city of 55,000 in the upper midwest region of the United States, was, until the late 1980s, largely untouched by the dramatic increase nationally in ESL[1] students (Olsen, 1993; Snow & Kamhi-Stein, 1998).

However, by 1989, the growing number of Southeast Asian Hmong students, in addition to other ESL students at UWEC, and the academic difficulties these students were encountering, brought the issue of providing appropriate institutional support for students with weak language proficiency to the attention of faculty, advisers, and other support service staff. It was clear that our institution was not meeting the needs of these ESL students (Bosher, 1992), a common situation in smaller U.S. colleges and universities. UWEC was caught in the ethical dilemma of admitting students

---

[1] In this chapter, *ESL* refers to foreign-born students who have attended one or more years of high school in the United States or Canada and consider either country to be their home, whether as refugees, immigrants, or naturalized citizens. *EFL* refers to international students in the United States or Canada who have completed their secondary education in their home countries and intend to return there upon completing college or postgraduate studies in the United States or Canada.

who were academically at risk but not providing them with the support they needed to be successful students.

Richard-Amato (1992) identified four key issues that many institutions with ESL populations must address to meet the needs of their NNS students:

1. lack of curricular guidelines and continuity of instruction

2. continued growth in the number of university ESL students

3. gaps between high school skills and university expectations of ESL students

4. limited academic success of university ESL students

These issues posed problems at UWEC. Our concern over how to address these issues and how best to provide appropriate ESL services resulted in an external audit (Bosher, 1992) of the university's existing EFL program for international students. This audit echoed Richard-Amato's warnings and recommended, among other things, the (a) development of new ESL courses specifically for ESL students; (b) development of a curriculum focused on integrating academic listening, vocabulary, speaking, reading, and writing skills; and (c) joining of academic content courses with ESL adjunct classes and tutoring. In short, UWEC needed to enlarge the scope of services provided to NNS students and develop "an academic bridge program for ESL students" that would "truly offer those students who are accepted the kind of preparation and support services needed to be academically successful" (Bosher, 1992, p. 15). As a direct result of this audit, the university began developing the CEP to address these issues.

Program Limitations and Goals

Despite a concern for immigrant ESL students by many faculty and staff, UWEC faced a significant handicap when it tried to create a new developmental program to meet their needs. Because there were few ESL students to work with each year (usually between 9–15), the university administration was unwilling to provide the financial resources to develop a new program, a lack of institutional commitment endemic to many campuses trying to improve the academic success of their ESL students (McNairy, 1996). The administration insisted that any new program make use of existing services and programs on campus. With this financial limitation, representatives from the EFL program, Academic Skills Center, American Ethnic Office, Admissions Office, Academic and Career Services, and Academic Advising began meeting to develop goals for a new, structured ESL program that would deal with issues raised by the external audit but still operate within the financial constraints set by the administration. Although the representatives brought different perspectives and agendas to the initial meetings, all agreed that there were ESL students on campus who were not being well served and recognized that a unified effort would be required if their needs were to be addressed.

First of all, it was seen as critical that the curriculum be academically relevant and that the ESL students see it as playing an important role in their academic success. This would be a difficult task, as ESL students who speak English fairly well and have graduated from U.S. or Canadian high schools have a tendency to assess their academic language proficiency unrealistically. Consequently, they are not always aware of and receptive to the need for more ESL or study skills instruction. These students frequently avoided classes with heavy language demands at the secondary level and hope to do the same in college. Often they believe that courses unrelated to their major, particularly English language classes, are unnecessary and, perhaps, even obstruct, rather than facilitate, their educational objectives. These students also frequently resent being put in ESL classes if they were already mainstreamed in high school.

A second goal was to develop a program that would not make ESL students dependent upon special assistance for the long-term but, rather, provide them with a solid foundation and appropriate learning strategies to prepare them for the academic demands they would be facing (Levitz & Noel, 1995).

Third, research clearly shows the importance of teaching study and learning skills in the context of courses in which students are enrolled (Levin & Levin, 1991; Robyak & Patton, 1977). Consequently, there was a desire to integrate, as much as possible, any support features that were instituted into the academic classes the students were taking.

Last, there was a desire to incorporate an emphasis on academic literacy, focusing on the more challenging context-reduced, cognitively demanding language tasks of formal schooling—the academic language needed to understand, analyze, and critique complex ideas (Cummins, 1984a). It was clear that weak language skills were a major source of difficulty for the ESL students at UWEC, and the CEP that was being developed needed to address and meet the language needs of these students in order to help them reach their academic goals.

Student Profile

UWEC requires all incoming students to take the University of Wisconsin English Placement Test (UWEPT) before enrolling. Any student with either a low UWEPT score (below 450) or an ACT Assessment® English score below 17 is required to take a remedial English writing course (English 099) before taking the required first-year English writing course (English 110).

Although relatively few in number, more students from linguistically diverse backgrounds began applying to UWEC beginning in the late 1980s. Most of the ESL students accepted at UWEC have been Southeast Asian (e.g., Cambodian, Laotian, Vietnamese, Hmong), the largest group being Hmong. In addition, students from Mexico, Central America, and Libya are also represented. It is this population that the CEP seeks to assist.

The L1 educational backgrounds of these CEP students tend to be varied and inconsistent. Although some can read and write in their native language, the majority use their L1 only for speaking socially; they lack L1 reading and writing skills. For the most part, the students have been in the United States for at least 4 years and have graduated from U.S. high schools, although clearly with shortcomings in English and academic skills. As more of these ESL students began enrolling at UWEC in the early 1990s, it was quickly realized that the vast majority—as many as 70% (Hisrich, Upton, & Stoffers, 1994) of those admitted who required remedial English composition—failed to complete the university-required freshman composition course (English 110), even by the end of their second year. In fact, most of these students dropped out after their first or second semester on campus.

With the start of the CEP in 1994, ESL students who do not test into English 110 are now placed in a special ESL section of remedial English (English 099), which is one of the courses in the CEP. This class provides the easiest means for comparing CEP students with the rest of the UWEC student body.

Freshman Profiles

Table 1 compares the ACT Assessment English scores, UWEPT scores, and high school percentile ranks of students placed into the CEP sections of English 099 with students placed in regular sections of English 099 during the fall semesters of 1994, 1995, 1996, and 1997. Table 2 compares the CEP sections with all freshman students.

As can be seen from Tables 1 and 2, the freshman students enrolled in the ESL sections of English 099 are at academic risk, as indicated by their weak ACT Assessment English and UWEPT scores. These ESL students have significantly lower placement scores (p < .001) compared to not only the average UWEC freshman but even to the average native-English-speaking (NS) student taking remedial English (English 099). In addition, these ESL students generally have an inability to evaluate and monitor their progress and to use resources sufficiently and effectively to promote their success (McNairy, 1996). These are clearly students at risk.

◈ DESCRIPTION

The CEP, an academic bridge program focusing on reading and writing for academic purposes, with additional work on vocabulary development and study skills, was developed to meet the needs of the students just described. The general concept and

TABLE 1. COMPARISON OF STANDARDIZED TEST SCORES AND HIGH SCHOOL RANK FOR STUDENTS IN CEP VERSUS REGULAR SECTIONS OF ENGLISH 099

Fall Semester: 1994, 1995, 1996, 1997	English 099 CEP Section (N = 46)	English 099 Regular Section (N = 71)	ANOVA P value
Mean ACT Assessment® English Score	13.1	15.0	<.001
Mean UWEPT Score	415	462	<.001
Mean High School Percentile Rank	60	54	ns*

*not significant

TABLE 2. COMPARISON OF STANDARDIZED TEST SCORES AND HIGH SCHOOL RANK FOR STUDENTS IN CEP SECTIONS OF ENGLISH 099 VERSUS ALL FIRST-YEAR STUDENTS

Fall Semester: 1994, 1995, 1996, 1997	English 099 CEP Section (N = 46)	All 1st-Year Students (N = 8353)	ANOVA P value
Mean ACT Assessment® English Score	13.1	22.4	<.001
Mean UWEPT Score	415	588	<.001
Mean High School Percentile Rank	60	72	<.010

name were adopted from the University of Minnesota's CEP,[2] but the program structure and curriculum were designed to meet UWEC's specific needs. Following the general recommendations of Snow & Brinton (1988), UWEC's 1-year program seeks to (a) engage students in intensive and extensive reading in college-level subject matter, (b) provide practice working with language to develop skills and strategies necessary for proficient writing, and (c) provide opportunities for the application of learning strategies to meaningful contexts through the use of adjunct courses connected to regular academic classes. The CEP curriculum also consists of reading and writing instruction specifically designed for ESL students, in addition to selected courses from various disciplines open to all other UWEC students. Table 3

TABLE 3. CEP FALL SEMESTER CURRICULUM

CEP Course Title	Course Description
English 099 Composition Fundamentals (3 credits)	Required by UWEC for all students with an ACT English Score below 17 (includes all CEP students). The English Department offers a section reserved only for ESL students but uses the same curriculum for all sections.
English 099 Adjunct Grammar and Reading Skills	This adjunct to English 099 provides intensive work on grammar and reading skills, using reading and writing assignments from English 099 as the content for the course.
Psychology 100 Introduction to Psychology (3 credits)	CEP students enroll in a regular section, which is open to all students at UWEC and is taught by an instructor with a strong background in working with ESL students (see Snow, 1997). This course was chosen because it meets General Education requirements for almost all majors at UWEC.
General Education 102 Study Skills in the Discipline Adjunct (1 credit)	This adjunct course to Psychology 100 is open to all UWEC students who are at academic risk and is taught by the Psychology 100 teacher. The focus is on the study skills needed to be successful in university-level classes; assignments and tests for Psychology 100 are used as the course content.
Math Elective (4–5 credits)	Students enroll in the mathematics course into which they placed as a result of the required math placement test given to all new students. UWEC has a general math requirement that all students must meet. Because the language demands are not as difficult in these math courses, CEP students are expected to begin working to meet their math requirements during their first semester.
Library and Media Education 110 Library Research Skills (1 credit)	CEP students are generally very weak in their understanding of how to use library resources for classroom assignments, including the use of computers for research. This class provides an introduction to the library while also giving them one more credit necessary for maintaining full-time student status.

---

[2] Information about the University of Minnesota's Commanding English Program can be found at http://www.gen.umn.edu/programs/ce/.

lists the specific courses CEP students take during their first semester on campus, with a brief description explaining the purpose and rationale for including each course in the program.

Courses taken during the second semester by CEP students are outlined in Table 4, with a description explaining the purpose and rationale for including each course in the program.

In addition to these courses, students are also provided with support services for coping with the academic and social demands of the university (McNairy, 1996), as outlined below.

◈ DISTINGUISHING FEATURES

Grants from the West Central Wisconsin Consortium (WCWC) were first used to help offset startup costs for the CEP, but all courses and services are now provided as a part of the programs and functions already established at the university. The CEP is able to operate with no specific budget due to the fact that it has been embraced by a broad cross-section of university offices, departments, faculty, and staff, who have assumed duties on behalf of the CEP as part of their regular responsibilities. The primary duties associated with this program are described below.

Recruitment and Admission

Having resolved to develop the CEP, the university decided to use it as a recruitment tool to increase minority enrollment at UWEC. Recruitment activities are year-round. This is primarily a joint effort between specific individuals in the Admissions and the

TABLE 4. CEP SPRING SEMESTER CURRICULUM

CEP Course Title	Course Description
English 100 Academic Reading and Writing for Non-native Speakers of English (3 credits)	This is a course for CEP students who, after completing English 099, are still not ready to take the required English 110 course: College Writing. Most CEP students take this course.
Geography 111 Human Geography (3 credits)	CEP students enroll in a regular section, which is open to all students at UWEC and is taught by an instructor with a strong background in working with ESL students. This course was chosen because it meets General Education requirements for almost all majors at UWEC.
General Education 103 Critical Thinking in the Discipline Adjunct (2 credits)	This course is an adjunct to Geography 111 and is limited to ESL students. Students focus on reading, note taking, test preparation, and study skills using the content and assignments for Geography 111.
Math/Science/ Humanities electives (4–8 credits)	Students are carefully advised and placed into courses they need to take to meet their major, minor, or General Education requirements. Most CEP students are only permitted to take 1XX-level courses during their second semester.

American Ethnic Offices assigned to work with minority populations. These two offices also consult with the associate director of Academic and Career Services and the director of ESL Programs when trying to determine the admissibility of students who are borderline in their qualifications. Recruitment efforts include visits to state and regional high schools known to have high populations of ESL students as well as regular contacts with high school counselors who work with ESL populations. Students admitted into the CEP are considered conditional admissions and must stay in and satisfactorily complete the requirements of the program in order to remain in good standing at the university.

Advising

Advising is carried out at several levels. Upon entering the university, students first meet with an academic advisor specifically assigned to work with CEP students. Students are provided an overview of the CEP and are assisted in the registration process. The student services coordinator in the American Ethnic Office and an advisor in the Academic Advising Office also meet regularly with these students to ensure they understand the program purposes and requirements and to assist the students in selecting appropriate courses for the subsequent semester. The director of ESL Programs communicates with the faculty advisers for all CEP students before registration begins in the spring semester to make sure they are all aware of the goals of the CEP and the special needs of students participating in the program.

Instruction

As already discussed, the language-oriented and academic support classes (e.g., English 099, English 100, General Education 103) are taught by trained ESL faculty and instructors. These instructors teach these classes either as part of their instructional load or on a fee-recovery basis. Academic courses (e.g., Psychology 100, Geography 111, Library and Media Education 110) are taught by faculty who have agreed to accept at-risk ESL students in their regular classes and are willing to make the extra effort to work with these students outside of class (Snow, 1997).

Monitoring

The progress of students participating in the CEP is monitored very closely, especially during the students' first two semesters on campus. Instructors for all of their classes report regularly on academic progress. Problems with study habits and poor quiz and test grades, for instance, are quickly noted and addressed immediately within the classes themselves, in tutoring sessions, or with students' academic advisers.

Tutoring

The CEP offers ESL students almost unlimited tutoring opportunities during their first year (Carreathers, Beekman, Coatie, & Nelson, 1996). The ESL program manager in the Academic Skills Center hires, trains, and supervises tutors. All students are assigned a tutor as a lab component of the English 099 class (fall semester) and English 100 class (spring semester), and all attend one or two hour-long sessions each week to work on individualized grammar programs. During this time they can also receive assistance with reading and writing assignments as needed.

Optional tutoring is also available for other course work. The majority of CEP students take advantage of this service.

Mentoring

Mentoring is an optional program that matches first-year CEP students with returning students of color to provide a role model, study partner, or simply someone with whom to share and discuss UWEC experiences (Carreathers et al., 1996). The number of contacts is decided mutually and varies. As an example, more than 70% of CEP students during the fall semester of 1996 met with a mentor an average of 15 times (about once a week) during the semester. The numbers have been comparable during other terms.

Communication

To facilitate communication between the wide network of instructors, advisers, tutors, mentors, and university officers involved with providing services to students in the CEP, representatives from each of the units involved meet on a regular basis to discuss and plan. The director of ESL Programs coordinates all of these efforts.

◈ PRACTICAL IDEAS

Design a Transition Program That Meets Degree Requirements Across Majors

Try to make as many courses in the transitional program as possible relevant to students' undergraduate degree programs. At UWEC, the psychology and human geography courses, which CEP students take along with their adjunct support courses, as well as the mathematics courses meet the General Education requirements for nearly all majors in all departments. The key point is that the courses supported by a transition program such as the CEP at UWEC should meet degree requirements for as many different majors as possible. Otherwise, students may perceive the courses they are taking as being irrelevant to them.

Have Students Meet Weekly With a Tutor

Tutoring is a particularly important component of the CEP. The CEP requires students to meet with a tutor weekly as part of the requirements for the two CEP English writing classes that they take, English 099 and English 110. This allows the instructors to tailor homework and language development exercises to the language needs of individual students. Tutors at UWEC are juniors and seniors who have done well in their English courses. For universities that have a graduate TESL program, a tutoring program such as this would work well and could be made even more cost effective by allowing TESL students to serve as tutors as part of a practicum or field experience requirement.

Make Tutoring Available for Content Courses

Tutoring for the content courses (e.g., psychology, human geography) is optional for CEP students. Because these courses have an adjunct course connected to them, all

CEP students generally are enrolled in the same section of the content course to facilitate instruction in the adjunct course. Early in the semester, a general announcement is made in the content class, soliciting students (who are at least sophomores with a grade point average above 3.5 and have demonstrated good study routines) to work as tutors for the CEP. This tutor is a classmate of the CEP student and is therefore already familiar with the lecture material and course assignments. The tutor meets weekly with pairs of CEP students to review and discuss material covered in the class. This tutoring arrangement has worked well, but it could easily be expanded or adapted to other contexts, especially those in which there is no supporting adjunct course. What might be more appropriate would be the development of study groups among all the students in the content class, into which CEP-type students could be mixed. The integration of such students into a university community exposes them to more strategies for reviewing and learning course material.

Consider a Less Structured Program for Students During Their Second Year

Because a committee of representatives from a wide number of offices and departments with no specific budget runs the CEP, the program has only been able to work with students during their first year on campus. Once students move out of programs like the CEP, they are no longer monitored and assisted to the same degree. Because the goal of such programs is to help students become fully integrated into the university community, this is not necessarily undesirable. Nevertheless, it is clear that these students are still at considerable academic risk even after their first year. A less structured, possibly optional, program that continued into these students' second year could prove extremely beneficial to them.

◈ CONCLUSION

The CEP at UWEC has been a successful academic bridge program for several reasons. First, the CEP provides the kind of academic preparation as well as the support services necessary to help at-risk ESL students gain the skills and achieve the personal expectations they need to succeed academically. The CEP is very structured, with students expected to take specific classes during their first year on campus. This allows faculty and advisors to closely monitor and assist students and respond quickly to problems students are experiencing before it is too late.

Second, students see the CEP as beneficial to their long-term academic success, as indicated by program evaluations. Most of the courses they take in the CEP meet graduation requirements. The few language and academic support classes they are expected to take either prepare them for or deal directly with and support the material they are studying in other classes. The language and study skills and strategies they are taught relate to the academic material they know they must learn to do well in their classes. We experience almost no trouble with attendance in these support classes because students recognize the value and importance of participating.

Last, the CEP helps ESL students become integrated into the university community. From the beginning, the CEP is structured to nurture relationships between students and their academic advisors, faculty advisors, and course instructors.

The students learn to seek help from the various offices across the campus. With the mentoring and tutoring program we provide, students have regular contact with other successful students who provide peer advice on ways to succeed at UWEC as well as how to deal with academic and personal issues.

As the success of the CEP at UWEC shows, ESL students do respond and learn to succeed when they are given the support they need. It goes without saying that colleges and universities across Canada and the United States differ in structure and mission, and that the capability and desirability of implementing a full-fledged transitional academic program for postsecondary ESL students such as those in the CEP would vary greatly among so many institutions.

Furthermore, the CEP is not a magical program. ESL students at UWEC still have many problems that make long-term success at the university a challenge. In many respects, they have to work harder than their NS counterparts to achieve corresponding success. What the CEP does do—and what universities and colleges are ethically bound to do—is provide the academic and language support ESL students need as they make the transition from high school to college, and it does this in such a way that students recognize the relevance of the program and take advantage of the help that is offered. The CEP at UWEC is but one good model to follow.

◈ CONTRIBUTOR

Thomas A. Upton received his MA in TESOL and PhD in Second Languages and Cultures Education from the University of Minnesota, in the United States. He is currently the director of the ESL program at Indiana University Purdue University Indianapolis and was the director of ESL and of the Commanding English Program at the University of Wisconsin-Eau Claire until 1998.

CHAPTER 8

Race, Gender, Class, and Academic ESL

Joan Lesikin

❖ INTRODUCTION

From my experience, I have observed that many ESL students are apprehensive about racial discrimination directed at them; they may view the United States as a racist country based on depictions in the media, yet have limited knowledge about the history of the U.S. Civil Rights Movement. They themselves may hold racist views. These same students seem moderately aware of sexism, sometimes noting gender role expectations in the United States similar to and, most especially, different from their own cultures. Some experiment with new English-speaking gender identities; others adhere strictly to their cultures' traditional gender role expectations. Nevertheless, many view sexism in any language as immutable. In addition to racial and gender distinctions, ESL students also become aware of class distinctions in U.S. society when newly arrived family members face limited employment, schooling, housing, healthcare, elderly care, and childcare opportunities because they are immigrants. Hence, race, gender, and class are highly relevant topics for academic ESL students and are, therefore, also delicate issues to which content-area instructors who teach mainstreamed ESL students need to be sensitive.

These reasons, combined with the desire to mainstream ESL students into the rigors of the academic core curriculum as soon as possible, support the university course described in this chapter, in which the upper level ESL reading and writing courses are linked with the general education (GE) course Racism and Sexism in the U.S., and the lower level ESL reading and writing courses are linked with the GE course Introduction to Sociology. (The core curriculum is a block of GE courses required of all degree-seeking students, designed to provide a solid foundation in the liberal arts.) The aim of this article is to give the reader an overview of the upper level ESL linkage with the GE course Racism and Sexism in the U.S.

Although the academic ESL program serves immigrants and international students, the issues of race, gender, and class that we explore and the ways in which we explore these issues are applicable and relevant to different English language students in a variety of settings. Few if any institutions in any culture are free of inequalities related to ethnic or racial background, gender, or socioeconomic class. In addition, Maher's (1985) reminder—that bringing issues of race, gender, class, and sexuality from the confines of women's studies and multicultural programs to other disciplines provides a contrast to the worldview expressed in the traditional academic disciplines—is pertinent. This view has reflected the experiences and aims of people in power, distorted or omitted the different experiences of minority and working-class women and men, and alienated students from identifying with traditional knowledge and traditional ways of conveying and testing that knowledge. By exploring these issues by means of a collaborative, cooperative, and interactive pedagogy, Teays (1996) notes, we put "multicultural awareness into practice" (p. 25) to effect change.

◈ CONTEXT

Immigrant and international students are admitted to the university on the basis of transcripts, class rank, and either Test of English as a Foreign Language scores (550) or Scholastic Aptitude Test scores (360 verbal, 380 math), with the exception of low-income immigrants entering our special programs, who have lower scores and receive extensive support services. All immigrant and international students are placed in the academic ESL program on the basis of an in-house writing and reading test, assessed by ESL faculty.

The academic ESL program design is based on the adjunct model of language instruction, in which language study is linked with the study of academic content "to better integrate the reading, writing, and study skill requirements of the two disciplines" (Snow & Brinton, 1988, p. 37). At each of our two ESL levels, students simultaneously take 3 hours of reading, 6 hours of writing, and 3 hours of a GE course, for a total of 12 hours each week, for which students receive six credits toward the diploma. In addition, students typically take a math or computer course. An additional 2-hour ESL writing workshop serves the most proficient ESL students concurrently enrolled in Freshman Composition.

◈ DESCRIPTION

Typically, one third of the 35 students in a GE course section of Racism and Sexism in the U.S. are ESL students; the other two thirds are from the general student population, which consists of multilingual and monolingual students from working- and middle-class U.S. backgrounds. The GE course instructor knows that ESL students are among those enrolled in the course, but the ESL program does not supply a list of these students.

The GE course instructor furnishes the ESL faculty with a copy of the syllabus, the list of assigned readings, handouts, tests, and assignments. However, the ESL faculty does not follow the GE course syllabus. Instead, we integrate some of the themes, one of the assignments, and some of the reading selections into the ESL linked courses.

In preparation, one of the ESL instructors visits the Racism and Sexism in the U.S. classroom during the first class session when the syllabus is reviewed. During the review, the instructor discusses what is expected of the students (e.g., homework assignments, testing, in-class participation) as well as grading policies, materials, and goals so that the ESL faculty can clarify and reinforce these expectations as needed.

The ESL Writing Component

The 6-hour advanced ESL writing link is a theme-based instructional workshop that focuses on the composing process: Students learn to free-write, write, revise, and edit drafts; improve their grammatical accuracy; and help peers to revise and edit their written pieces. It is intended to help students develop fluency and accuracy in writing and achieve the ability to manipulate advanced-level English sentence structures by developing their competencies in lexis, morphology, and syntax.

The course encompasses (a) writing activities, such as summaries of readings, paraphrases of key paragraphs, critiques of readings, in- and out-of-class essays, and revised and edited works; (b) reading activities, such as analysis of the different rhetorical patterns used by native-English-speaking writers, prereading activities for reading assignments, reading, and discussion preceding writing; (c) minilessons on learning, writing, revising, editing, and grammar; (d) group work involving discussing, reading, viewing, writing, revising, and editing (not necessarily in that order) with peers; (e) self-, peer, and instructor assessments; and (f) information gathering through student research, instructor- and student-supplied texts, the media, and personal interviews.

The suggested texts for the writing course are the anthology used in the Racism and Sexism in the U.S. course; the *Longman Dictionary of Contemporary English* (Quirk et al., 1987); a writing textbook containing samples of authentic expository essays, discussions of different rhetorical modes with corresponding writing samples, a review of basic grammar items, discussions on sentence structure, vocabulary, and word forms, such as Oshima and Hogue's (1999) *Writing Academic English*; and a course packet of thematically related short readings.

By the end of the semester, we hope students are able to

- express critically in writing their ideas drawn from readings on race, gender, and class and relate those ideas to their own world experience

- write well-organized essays in response to a variety of assigned prompts

- write comprehensible and logical summaries and paraphrases of assigned readings that make use of advanced-level structures and vocabulary

- use advanced-level sentence structures and vocabulary in their essay writing

- apply editing strategies

The ESL Reading Component

The 3-hour reading link is an instructional workshop that focuses on intensive reading and vocabulary development. It is intended to help students read at the college level and to provide depth and background knowledge to the GE course themes.

The course includes (a) minilessons on reading- and vocabulary-building strategies and analyzing figurative speech; (b) intensive reading to comprehend, guess meaning in context, find detailed information, paraphrase and summarize information, and infer meaning; (c) discussions and writing in relation to texts by students relating their ideas and experiences and evaluating situations, events, language, and characters in texts; (d) writing responses in the form of short essays, comprehension exercises, or response journals; (e) instruction and use of library resources for research; and (f) collaborative work in which students read and respond together.

The suggested texts for the reading course, besides the dictionary, as in the writing link, consist of three books that are graded in level of difficulty and progress from narrative to expository texts. The first two are either biography or fiction, and the third is an anthology of essays. As the reading instructor, I presently use Halsell's (1996) autobiography, _In Their Shoes_; Griffin's (1960) autobiography, _Black Like Me_; and an anthology of essays, _Women and Men_ (Tarvers, 1992). I have also used Tan's (1989) _The Joy Luck Club_ and King's (1996) _The Green Mile_, and, instead of an anthology, culled essays from a variety of sources, including the GE course text.

At the end of the semester, students should be able to

- analyze paragraph and essay development

- use a broader English vocabulary through context cueing, dictionary use, and word analysis

- summarize and paraphrase reading passages

- analyze figurative language (e.g., idioms, metaphors and similes, analogies, allusions)

- read an unabridged, thematically-related, college-level expository English prose text (2,200–3,000 words in length) and successfully answer comprehension and short essay questions that emphasize inference

- use library resources to research topics

- discuss assigned readings intelligibly and productively

◈ DISTINGUISHING FEATURES

Linking Courses to Facilitate a Smooth Entry Into the Mainstream

ESL students can succeed in a mainstream GE course, such as Racism and Sexism in the U.S., while developing academic English language skills because the ESL links focus on language, academic skills, and content information specifically geared and immediately applicable to the GE course. In our ESL links, students gain background knowledge to help them understand the larger U.S. historical, social, political, and cultural contexts of what they are studying in the GE course—what U.S. students typically know from their own experiences. This knowledge is gained through the ESL students' greater amount of reading, writing, and discussion on selected topics. In addition, the ESL links relate the topics to students' present lives and cultural backgrounds so that U.S. issues become universal issues. Connections to the students are made through pre-, during, and postreading and prewriting collaborative activities, such as interviews, responses to worksheet prompts, research, and questionnaires on issues culled from readings. These activities ask students to draw comparisons to their own cultures or to express their views from different stances: as women or men; as coming from a particular social class or culture; as immigrants, parents, or children.

Collaboration Between Course Instructors

Although the reading, writing, and GE course instructors teach in their own self-contained classrooms, they all maintain the thematic focus on race, gender, and class and collaborate to help prepare ESL students for mainstream work. For instance, late in the semester, ESL reading and writing instructors collaborate on having students write a research paper on a self-selected topic as an expansion of an assigned position paper for the Racism and Sexism in the U.S. course. The students must find at least three articles to support their position for the research paper, even though they are not required to do so for the GE course position paper. The reading instructor arranges for a librarian to instruct the class in using online library search engines in the library's computer-equipped classroom and then assists students in their searches. Students conduct their research using library resources, such as periodical indexes and online services. The writing instructor then works with students to help them incorporate their findings, along with appropriate citations and references, into the expanded paper. It is this paper that each ESL student hands in for the Racism and Sexism in the U.S. class.

Another instance of collaboration is the linking of the reading and writing courses' midterm and final exams. The linked ESL course instructors select one reading to be used for testing in both courses. Throughout the semester, our intent is to have students apply to their writing the content information, vocabulary, and insights they acquire from making sense of a reading; therefore, for the midterm and final testing, the reading selection for the reading exam functions as the source for writing prompts for the corresponding writing exam. In our experience, students also suffer less anxiety with this combined approach than when taking two separate exams. We also facilitate student collaboration in preparing for the two exams by distributing the reading one week beforehand. Students may not ask for instructor assistance but can confer with each other about the reading, brainstorm potential writing prompts, or practice writing in response.

At a more informal collaborative level, the ESL reading and writing instructors sometimes share lesson plans and materials to augment them. For example, the writing instructor might ask the reading instructor to assign a reading on a particular topic or viewpoint because she perceives high student interest or the need for more knowledge for effective writing. Similarly, as the reading instructor, I might arrange with the writing instructor to supply some essay prompts from my assignments and discussions of a book. Together, we may need to adjust the due dates for completing the essay or the book, but this type of collaboration gives students more writing prompt options and an opportunity to write a more formal piece than would be available in the reading class.

Topic Selection by Students

At the beginning of the writing course, students in groups self-select seven topics of interest from a topic-selection sheet (see Figure 1). These topics then frame the ESL reading and writing links, giving students some control over the ESL curriculum. As the level leader, I cull topics for the selection sheet from the GE course textbook, which presently is Rothenberg's (1998) *Race, Class, and Gender in the United States: An Integrated Study*, and another textbook, McClean's (1999) *Solutions for the New Millennium: Race, Class, and Gender*, and include space for student topics. We find

Directions

As a group, select seven topics from the list below. You may add other topics if you wish. List them in order of interest, starting with 1 for the most interesting topic, 2 for the next most interesting topic, and so on, until you have selected seven. Write your rank number in the blank next to the topic.

When you have finished, have a group member write the seven topics on the blackboard, using only the topic number. For example, if your group chose Number 3 (Understanding Racism, Sexism, and Class Privilege) as the most interesting topic, then you would write 3 at the top of the list, and so on, until you have listed your seven topics. Then, as a class, we will compare lists and reach agreement on the seven topics we will study this semester. This will include exploring many of these topics in relation to our own cultures.

Topics

___ 1. **The Social Construction of Difference: Race, Class, Gender, and Sexuality**
The ways in which race, glass, gender, and sexuality have been socially constructed in the United States as *difference* in the form of hierarchy

___ 2. ***Us* and *Them*: Becoming an American**
What it means to be a citizen, an American, and an immigrant in the United States

___ 3. **Understanding Racism, Sexism, and Class Privilege**
What it means to be a racist, a sexist, or a privileged person in the United States

___ 4. **The Economics of Race, Class, and Gender in the United States**
Statistics and analyses that demonstrate the impact of race, class, and gender difference on people's lives

___ 5. **Many Voices, Many Lives: Some Consequences of Racial, Gender, and Class Inequality**
Articles, poems, and stories of glimpses into the lives of women and men of different ethnic and class backgrounds, expressing their sexuality and cultures in different ways

___ 6. **How It Happened: Race and Gender Issues in U.S. Law**
Examination of the important aspects of the history of subordinated groups in the United States by focusing on important documents that address race and gender issues in U.S. law since the beginning of the Republic

___ 7. **Creating and Maintaining Hierarchies: Stereotypes, Ideology, Language, Violence, and Social Control**
Suggestions about how racism, sexism, homophobia, and class privilege are perpetuated in contemporary U.S. society

___ 8. **Sex, Gender, Roles, and Family Life**
Glimpses into the impact of racism, sexism, and class inequality on the family life of women and men of different ethnic and class backgrounds

___ 9. **Race, Class, and Gender in the Arts: Music, Literature, the Visual Arts, Television, and Film**
A glimpse into how the arts and the media portray issues related to race, class, and gender in the United States

(continued on p. 97)

___ 10. **Revisioning the Future**
      Suggestions for moving beyond racism, classism, and sexism

___ 11. (suggested topic) _____

      _____

___ 12. (suggested topic) _____

      _____

Figure 1. Writing Class Topic Selection Sheet (Adapted from Rothenberg, 1998, and McClean & Lyles, 1993).

that brief explanations accompanying each topic help students make their selections. Group work on the first day also serves to give us feedback on the students' abilities at oral communication and group work.

Framing and Pacing: One Topic, One Essay

The student-selected topics drive the content for both ESL links. In the writing link, a formal essay ends each topic. Both courses begin with the students' first choice and move to the next topic when the writing instructor assigns the formal essay. Therefore, the reading and writing instructors collaborate to pace readings so that students in the reading class have sufficient time to complete reading assignments in order to incorporate what they have read into their essays if necessary. Typically the reading instructor starts the subsequent topic while students are completing a second draft for the previous topic.

Instructor-Initiated Prompts for Readings

To get students to read book-length texts intensively and apply higher level skills to their responses, we give them assignment sheets containing prompts, such as those used for Griffin's (1960) *Black Like Me* (see Figure 2).

Testing and Other Assessment Strategies

Testing and Placement

At midterm, the reading that is chosen to formally assess and evaluate students is 1,500–2,200 words in length; the reading used at the end of the semester is longer: 2,200–3,000 words. Students may bring the reading to both exams as long as it is a clean copy, that is, with no writing or markings added. Typically, the reading exams, made in-house, contain comprehension exercises and short essay questions. Reading instructors may also use an additional evaluative tool, such as a standard multiple-choice test. To pass the reading course, students must meet the following three criteria:

1. achieve passing scores on the two final reading exams
2. complete the required course work
3. maintain satisfactory attendance and participation in class

For the writing exam component, writing instructors design prompts to test the students' ability to respond and react to the issues presented in the reading selection

Directions

Below are reading assignments based on diary dates from Griffin's *Black Like Me* and questions that correspond to each reading. Be sure to complete the reading assignment before answering the corresponding question. After reading, respond to the assigned question in your own words. Take care in writing your responses and reactions.

Responses should be typed double-spaced or written neatly on alternate lines on one side only of a ruled sheet of notebook paper. Your responses to each prompt should be answered in complete sentences and as fully as possible. The length of responses will vary.

Diary Reading Assignment	Writing Assignment
October 28:	Why did Griffin decide to become a Negro?
October 29:	State the reaction of each: George Levitan, Adelle Jackson, Mrs. Griffin, Griffin.
October 30:	What was the purpose of the lunch?
November 1:	Describe Griffin's experience.
November 8:	Write a summary of the events in this section.
November 10–12:	(a) Define *economic injustice*.
	(b) Was the bus trip to Dillard University an example of economic injustice or another kind of injustice? Explain.
November 14:	(a) Describe *southern justice* from the Negroes' viewpoint. Then explain it from the Southern Whites' viewpoint.
	(b) In the Greyhound Bus station, Griffin encounters "the hate stare." What is it? Describe Griffin's reaction to it.
	(c) Describe the atmosphere in Mississippi that Griffin encounters.
	(d) Define *legalized injustice*, according to P. D. East.
	(e) Why did P. D. East's newspaper fail?
November 15:	Who does Griffin fault for perpetuating racism? Why?
November 16:	(a) What was the purpose of the literacy tests?
	(b) Rewrite the dedication to *For Men of Good Will* to be inclusive of both women and men.
	(c) Explain what Griffin means when he writes, "In these matters, the Negro has seen the backside of the white man too long to be shocked."
November 19:	Griffin lectures to the young driver in his late twenties about the plight of the Negro. Summarize his explanation in 50 words or less.
November 24:	(a) What does the sawmill worker mean by saying "Go ahead and eat the bread—but work and maybe someday we'll have butter to go with it"?
	(b) Explain how the two great arguments for segregation are "smoke screens."

(continued on p. 99)

	(c) Why does staying with the family in the swamp make Griffin feel such sorrow?
November 25:	What are the two things the Negroes in Montgomery feared?
November 27:	Write a one-sentence summary.
November 28:	(a) How did Griffin feel returning to white society?
	(b) The last sentence in the chapter seems to be missing the word "white." Where and why?
November 29:	Griffin asks, "Was it worth trying to show the one race what went on behind the mask of the other?" Write a response.
April 2:	(a) Why do you think the people of Mansfield remained silent?
	(b) Explain what Griffin means by "the slightest kindness on the part of anyone becomes a sort of bravery."
	(c) In your opinion, was the effigy hanging the work of "outsiders" or townspeople? Explain.
Epilogue:	(a) Describe briefly the stereotyped role of the "good Negro."
	(b) The white middle-aged boss told Griffin, "You better show us some teeth." What did he mean?
	(c) Explain the meaning of *character assassination* and why it was feared.
	(d) Explain *entrapment*.
	(e) Griffin writes, "In spite of everything, however, those days of the early and mid-sixties were full of hope." Explain why. He also writes that problems and frustrations still remained. Explain some of them.

FIGURE 2. Excerpt of Assignment Sheet for *Black Like Me* (Griffin, 1960).

and to relate these ideas to real-life situations, using the specific rhetorical pattern required by the prompt. The four criteria for passing the writing course are

1. competence in writing, as demonstrated by scores of at least a B on the last two in-class and last two out-of-class essay assignments

2. completion of required course work

3. satisfactory attendance and class participation

4. a score of at least a B on the final essay test

Students with grades of B or C place into freshman English and the ESL Writing Workshop; students who receive an A place into freshman English and have the option of taking the ESL Writing Workshop.

Student Self-Assessment

At midterm, student self-assessment for reading and writing is intended to stimulate students to think and make decisions about their own learning. By completing an instructor-made questionnaire, or one developed by the instructor and students, students (a) evaluate their reading and writing growth, homework, class participation, and attendance and (b) set specific goals for the remainder of the semester. Each student then meets with each instructor to discuss the self-assessment and to receive the instructor's evaluation and placement recommendation.

Ongoing Assessment

Assessment is ongoing in both linked ESL classes through instructor and student feedback, using several different approaches. In class and during office hours, writing instructors provide written feedback that focuses on making students' oral and written production comprehensible, complete, and logical. They hold individual and group writing conferences and facilitate students' peer and self-assessment sessions to reinforce writing, grammar, and editing skills.

In the linked ESL reading class, in-class, graded cloze procedures that progress from text deletions of every ninth word to deletions of every sixth are used to check comprehension, provide reinforcement of structures, and practice reading for meaning across sentence boundaries. Student pairs completing ancillary materials and group checks of homework provide peer feedback opportunities. Instructor feedback is supplied orally during discussions and in written form as well as by means of grades (e.g., excellent, satisfactory, unsatisfactory, incomplete) of written homework and class work.

◈ PRACTICAL IDEAS

Interactions With Texts

Encourage the Use of Highlighters

One technique to facilitate reading and vocabulary development throughout the semester is to have students use colored markers (highlighters)—one yellow and one pink—to mark text. They use the yellow highlighter to mark unfamiliar words or expressions as they read so as not to interrupt their reading; in this way, they can return to any marked item at a natural break in the reading to either use a dictionary or examine the language context more closely. Students use the pink highlighter to mark the margin alongside incomprehensible passages so that they can quickly refer to the passage in class sessions devoted to unraveling them. Teaching students to count paragraphs and lines within paragraphs helps others in the class locate the same passage quickly.

Promote Active Reading

Encourage students to read homework prompts before and during reading; the prompts provide comprehension cues because they supply some text information and a purpose for reading. Invite students to write in their books as they read to help them recall their reactions or to revisit a passage. In addition, for in-class reading, tasks might be assigned to be done with a partner before, during, and after a reading to raise students' awareness of a topic and to provide a reading purpose.

Help Build Vocabulary

To help students develop their vocabulary, have them select a designated number of unfamiliar words, define them, and use them in a sentence of their own making that matches the same meaning of the word in the reading. For example, in "Some women in a sexist society adopt the views of the male oppressor" (Romano, 1993,

NJ1), a student might be asked to use the word *adopt* similarly in a sentence to mean "to take up and make one's own," rather than "to take into one's family through legal means and raise as one's own child," or some other meaning.

Provide Assignment Choices

Besides instructor-made questions for a particular reading, use lists of prompts to elicit personal reactions to books and essays, as in Figure 3. The intention is to have students choose the type of response and the passage that most interests them. These types of prompts work especially well after students build experience through instructor-facilitated class discussions and respond to instructor-initiated prompts. Students might also be encouraged to write longer reactions; in our setting, we guide students with directions such as "The reaction part should be at least 50 words in length" and provide a model by doing one or two written form together as a class. We also share the responses of classmates by either posting some online or on the bulletin board, or by giving them as handouts.

Establish Student-Initiated Homework Review

There never seems to be enough time in the reading link to introduce and practice reading strategies, have students work together on difficult readings, and review homework; therefore, consider limiting the examination of homework to 20 minutes and to those items students choose to discuss. Students work together in groups of three or four and may ask other classmates for help as well when needed, knowing that the instructor will also look at their homework.

◈ CONCLUSION

The adjunct language learning model is not without drawbacks, the most serious being for language instructors. Integrating content materials with language teaching aims demands a significant commitment of language instructors' time and energy. They must familiarize themselves with the learning materials of the content course, develop language teaching materials based on that course content, and provide students with feedback on the language content as well as on the quality of that content (though to a lesser degree with the latter).

---

1. How did I feel about (a particular experience, thought, or idea)?
2. What did (a particular experience, thought, or idea) remind me of?
3. What might I have experienced, thought, or felt in a similar circumstance? What would I have done differently?
4. What were my first impressions? How did I feel after I finished reading the section?
5. What was positive and negative about what I read?
6. What did I learn? How could I apply what I learned to my own life?
7. What questions remain after reading the section?

FIGURE 3. Sample Prompts for Student Selection of Reading Passages

Content instructors must be willing to share their reading, pedagogical, and testing materials with the ESL instructors and discuss with them their methods of teaching. They must be willing to open up their classrooms so the language instructor can attend lectures.

The administration also faces serious challenges. It needs to provide release time for faculty development and weekly meetings to encourage collaboration among faculty from across disciplines. It also requires a stable ESL staff, familiar with the adjunct model and with faculty in other disciplines, to effect the necessary collaboration; otherwise, faculty development becomes burdensome and costly.

However, there are many benefits to the adjunct model. ESL and GE instructors get to collaborate with colleagues from different disciplines, consult with one another on students' progress, and recommend needed intervention. The ESL specialist has the chance to engage students with cognitively demanding subject matter and work with students so engaged. The GE course instructor gets to teach ESL students who are eager to learn about U.S.-centered information, practices, beliefs, theories, and ideas, and are capable of offering their U.S. classmates a different and equally interesting perspective. ESL students benefit from familiarity with the same instructors and students, which creates a cohesive, supportive group of learners and has been shown to increase motivation and lessen anxiety. The trust that develops seems to allow ESL students to take risks as part of their learning process and to speak up in the GE class with their U.S. classmates. It is not surprising, then, that retention rates for ESL students are greater using the adjunct model of language instruction (Guyer & Peterson, 1988).

◈ CONTRIBUTOR

Joan Lesikin, a teacher trainer and academic ESL teacher, is interested in the social implications of educational text materials and L2 teaching practices. Her recent publications include "Gender in Public Life: Pedagogy for ESL" (*Issues in Gender, Language Learning, and Classroom Pedagogy*, 2001) and "Determining Social Prominence: A Methodology for Uncovering Gender Bias in ESL Textbooks" (*College ESL*, 1998), for which she was awarded the 2001 Fred W. Malkemes Prize.

CHAPTER 9

Escape From Alcatraz: Breaking Away From the ESL Island

Joe Greenholtz

◈ INTRODUCTION

The UBC-Ritsumeikan Academic Exchange Programme (AEP) is a joint venture between two partner universities: the University of British Columbia (UBC) in Vancouver, Canada, and Ritsumeikan University, in Kyoto, Japan. The AEP brings 100, mostly 2nd-year, students to UBC for an academic year to do content course work for academic credit in an integrated environment. This chapter describes the students and the educational and sociocultural program provided for them, with emphasis on the structures established to mainstream them in the UBC environment and avoid the ghettoization so common with island programs.[1] The academic components, particularly the content-based language study and other course work, are described, as are the residential and extracurricular elements of the program.

◈ CONTEXT

The Japanese participants in the UBC-Ritsumeikan AEP are, for the most part, 2nd-year students of Ritsumeikan University, a private university with two campuses in the Kyoto area and a student population of roughly 30,000. AEP students are drawn from all of the university's eight faculties: Law, Economics, Business Administration, Letters, Social Science, Science and Engineering, International Relations, and Policy Science. The AEP, now in its 11th year, attracts an average of 150 applicants annually for the 100 available spaces. Students are accepted into the program on the basis of their academic performance, their Test of English as a Foreign Language (TOEFL) scores, and selection interviews. Successful candidates' incoming TOEFL scores range between the three or four students at the extremes (lows of 480 and highs of 580), with the majority averaging somewhere around 520. UBC's admission standard for Arts undergraduates is TOEFL 580 (570 in the Science faculties), which presented some initial challenges in achieving the program's goal of providing students with for-credit study in the university's mainstream. Most of the Japanese participants are studying abroad for the first time, although up to 10% in any given

---

[1] An island program is one in which visiting students are engaged in noncredit ESL study in isolation from the rest of the campus community.

year will have had some experience (of several weeks to a year) in an ESL or English-language homestay environment. As is typical of most Japanese university students, most of them have never experienced English other than as a subject to be studied in order to pass examinations. This puts them under significant pressure when they try to cope with the demands of their course-related reading load and assignments, and, simultaneously, with the sociocultural and linguistic demands of residence and cultural adaptation outside their native country.

On arrival in September, students are given an entry proficiency interview, using the Foreign Service Interview (FSI) protocol, and a writing test, which is modeled on TOEFL's Test of Written English but graded on internal criteria. They also do a self-rating, based on the Canadian Language Benchmarks (CLB) criteria. Their highest incoming TOEFL scores are also recorded. These ratings are repeated in mid-April, just before the students return to Japan, to measure language proficiency gains over the course of the program (see the Appendix).

One may ask why the AEP is called an exchange program if only Japanese students are coming from Japan to Canada. The AEP's mandate is to integrate the Ritsumeikan students with their UBC peers as fully as possible within the academic, sociocultural, and linguistic domains of university life. It is this mandate that provides the primary impetus for mainstreaming the Japanese students because the AEP's vision of what constitutes an exchange does not necessarily involve physically interchanging the participating students. The AEP is promoted on the UBC campus as an opportunity for UBC students to participate in an international exchange without leaving home. Although the AEP anticipated UBC's present goal of providing all students with an international experience as part of their undergraduate program by 10 years, the program dovetails with UBC's notion of internationalization, as described in the university's 2000 vision statement.

UBC and Ritsumeikan students are integrated in campus residences, including in Ritsumeikan-UBC House (Rits House), which was built for the program, and in academic work. Classroom integration is discussed more fully below.

Rits House holds 200 students in suites with four single bedrooms (called *quads*) and shared kitchen and living space. Although the quads were originally allocated to two Ritsumeikan and two UBC students, the Ritsumeikan students' desire to live outside such a densely Japanese atmosphere, and the AEP's desire to include as many UBC students as possible in the residential experience, led to an increasing number of Ritsumeikan students being placed in single-student residences outside Rits House. The prevailing pattern in Rits House is now to have one Ritsumeikan student share a quad with three UBC students. Rits House, with its rich social and cross-cultural programming provided by the AEP program office, Housing Residence Life Advisory staff, and the students' own house council, serves as the hub of the program. It is the locus of a variety of events, such as an annual Open House, which involve the participation of members of the greater university community.

In addition to its residential functions, Rits House is also central to the academic program. There are classrooms on the second floor and RitsLab, a 20-station multimedia lab, in the basement. Each RitsLab station is equipped with a networked Macintosh computer, with a direct ethernet connection, and a Sony language-lab module, with audiocassette deck and headphones. Two stations share a video monitor and VCR, which can also be programmed from the teacher's console for whole-class viewing of materials. RitsLab is the site of all lab sections for courses offered by the Language and Literacy Education Department (LLED) and the Introduction to Canadian Studies (ICS) course. These courses are more fully described below. Students are taught and encouraged to work with a variety of software and to do Web-based research. In-class presentations have become increasingly sophisticated over the years, with highly polished PowerPoint® presentations emerging as the standard. After hours, all residents of the building are free to use RitsLab for computing and Internet access. Although every residence room at UBC has a direct ethernet connection to the UBC network, not every student brings a personal computer, or a printer, to the residence.

Ritsumeikan students make the transition into the North American academic environment by spending their first term in two content courses taught by instructors from the LLED, in the Faculty of Education. They also take the ICS course, taught primarily by the Faculty of Arts, which gives them an overview of contemporary Canadian life. The two LLED courses were originally sheltered, but 4 years ago, all restrictions were removed and the courses became available on the general UBC registration system.

The Japanese students' first-term schedule calls for 11.5 contact hours per week, in recognition of the fact that course preparation, reading, and assignments take much longer for these students than for students admitted to UBC under general admission circumstances. In addition, the relatively light timetable permits students to pursue community-placement activities that form part of their academic requirements as well as a wide variety of volunteer activities, ranging from acting as teaching assistants in Japanese-language classes to helping out in daycare centers and care facilities for the elderly. Language-exchange arrangements are also extremely popular, with many of the students having more than one partner.

In the second term, the LLED courses continue, although with substantially different content, and two other courses in the Faculty of Arts are added. These courses, Arts Studies (ASTU) 201 and 202, were created for the AEP and have always been open to the general UBC student population. ASTU 202 is also cross-listed as Geography 281. The ASTU courses were jointly created (and are jointly recreated every year) by instructors from each university and are team taught each year.

The fact that the ASTU courses have always been open to UBC students initially created a hurdle in mainstreaming the Ritsumeikan students, as there was some reluctance to permit international students who did not satisfy UBC admissions requirements to mix in the classroom with UBC students. There was concern that course content would have to be diluted to permit the Ritsumeikan students to keep up, at the expense of the UBC students. However, a creative solution, in which the students' first-term averages are given equal weight with their TOEFL scores, has been in place since 1997 and has proven to be an effective compromise. More will be said about the adaptation of the TOEFL threshold in the following section.

◈ DESCRIPTION

The AEP's academic philosophy is derived from Mohan's (1986) content-based language learning approach. To reduce the content-based approach to its most basic terms, it posits that language acquisition follows as a natural consequence of studying content of intrinsic interest to the language learner.

Of the three courses taken by the Ritsumeikan students in their first term at

UBC, two—Language Field Experience (LLED 206) and Language Across the Curriculum (LLED 226)—have been approved for UBC credit by the University Senate. The third course, ICS, awards Ritsumeikan, but not UBC, credit (i.e., credit is awarded for transfer back to Ritsumeikan University, but the course does not appear on the students' UBC transcripts). Because the two LLED courses and the ICS course are fundamentally different in almost all respects, they will be described separately.

ICS is a semester-long course consisting of a 1-hour weekly lecture attended by all 100 AEP participants, followed by a 90-minute tutorial. There is also a 90-minute lab session taught by LLED teaching assistants (TAs) once a week. One objective of the course is to provide students with an overview of contemporary Canadian society. The second objective is to permit students to focus their studies on something related to their majors. Each of four faculty members delivers a 3-week block of lectures on one of the following topics: Canadian social issues, law and politics, economics, and culture and the arts. The tutorials concentrate on one of these four areas (each student selects an area of interest) so that, even though the topic of the lecture and the particular focus of the tutorial may not always be in synch, the tutorial structure permits the group to approach the lecture from the perspective of the specialist focus. Thus, a lecture on arts and culture can be approached by the economics tutorial from the perspective of mounting cultural events in Canadian cities with limited population bases or of attracting (or keeping) major talent against the pull of the stronger U.S. dollar and the prestige of succeeding in the United States. The law and politics tutorial could approach the same lecture block from the perspective of whether culture should be subject to the provisions of the North America Free Trade Agreement or whether it should be exempt from competition statutes in order to allow Canada to protect its cultural industries from powerful U.S. media conglomerates.

The lab sessions are adjunct in the sense that the research skills, vocabulary, reading, and listening strategies pertinent to the study of that particular discipline are examined and practiced. The fact that ICS is not for UBC credit permits the AEP to use these sessions to provide specialized language support, as ESL instruction is not eligible for credit at UBC. There is, of course, generalization from the strategies learned and practiced in the ICS labs to L2 learning in the content-based curriculum.

UBC Courses

Like ICS, the LLED courses deal with aspects of contemporary Canadian culture. However, unlike ICS, LLED courses carry three UBC credits and, as such, are governed by the same academic criteria as other course offerings at the university. This specifically precludes the teaching of ESL, despite the fact that the courses were created for the AEP and originally designated as sheltered courses open only to Ritsumeikan students. For the past several years they have been open to the general UBC population and would be of particular interest to international students. Although we have been unable to attract more than a handful of UBC students each year, domestic or international, the presence of even one or two non-Japanese students in a section dramatically alters the dynamics of the interaction among students. As a result, the AEP will continue to try to improve its recruiting strategies to bring the first-term LLED courses further into the mainstream.

Both LLED courses consist of a weekly lecture, tutorial, and lab session, each 90 minutes long. Students enroll in one of five sections of 20 students each. The LLED course titles, a historical legacy, are somewhat misleading or, rather, uninformative. Language Field Experience (LLED 206) provides a theoretical framework within which students can contextualize intercultural communication and the task of defining one's identity with respect to culture of origin and adopted culture, in this case mainstream Canadian society, as well as instruction in research methods. The course addresses issues such as the influence of sociocultural forces on interactions within and among communities, cultural identity and values, prejudice, and competence in intercultural communication. Students research intercultural communication through community-based volunteer and work placements, observing and reporting on their own interactions and the interactions of others in those settings. It would be no exaggeration to say that immigration is one of contemporary Canada's defining forces and multiculturalism one of its defining features. Immigration is a particularly salient feature of the Greater Vancouver area. Known locally as the Lower Mainland, Vancouver is one of the most cosmopolitan cities on the continent, with over 50% of the students in the public school system designated as ESL learners. The variety and expression of ethnicities come as a shock to the Japanese AEP students, accustomed as they are to the relative uniformity and homogeneity, on a macro level, of Japanese society. Classroom work provides instruction in field research techniques and a context for understanding and framing the field work. This combination is particularly important when students are asked to attempt techniques, approaches, and content that are beyond the boundaries of their educational schemata. That AEP students can meet the challenge of producing high-quality work was demonstrated when several students were selected to present their research at the annual British Columbia Teachers of English as an Additional Language conference in February 2001.

LLED 206a's companion course, LLED 226a, Language Across the Curriculum, offers a variety of content that continues to evolve over time, depending on the instructors' inclinations and students' interests. LLED 226a (offered in the first term) has traditionally used the short stories and literature of Canada's native and immigrant communities to explore themes such as generational conflict, multicultural education, the struggle for identity, the impact of colonization, gay and lesbian subcultures, and institutional racism.

In recent years, students have been offered opportunities to pursue studies in creative thinking and media. For example, in Explorations in Creativity and Innovation, students learn how to overcome obstacles to creative thinking through journal writing, exercises, and activities. The course examines various theories of creativity and innovation and how they relate to the concept of problem solving in the arts, business, media, technology, and urban design, using readings, videos, problem-solving exercises, role plays, workshops, guest speakers, and other research resources.

Introduction to Popular Media is an introduction to print media (e.g., magazines, newspapers, books) and electronic media (e.g., radio, TV, movies, the music industry). The course is intended to deepen knowledge of these media, introduce the terminology needed to communicate in the various media industries, and increase awareness of issues and trends surrounding media. The first part of the course introduces four elements: production, distribution, exhibition, and finance. Students select a medium of interest and develop a research project on one aspect of that medium.

These courses, in addition to providing content study, are also designed to bring students up to speed on the structure and requirements of UBC course work, laying the groundwork for greater integration in the second term.

In the second term, the Ritsumeikan students' course load increases from three to a minimum of four (maximum of five) full-time courses. Students who have demonstrated the ability to succeed in course work during the first semester (see the following section) move further into the mainstream of UBC academic life, with an average of 15% (and rising) becoming eligible to take courses outside the AEP from the UBC calendar. The remaining students continue with the second half of the LLED curriculum.

In either case, two courses created for the AEP—Canada, Japan and the Pacific: Cultural Studies (ASTU 201) and Canada, Japan and the Pacific: Political, Economic and Geographical Perspectives (ASTU 202)—are compulsory. Ritsumeikan Students who take regular UBC courses in the second semester have the option of dropping an equivalent number of LLED courses in any combination that yields a minimum of 12 credits (i.e., four courses).

It took a number of years before the AEP was able to gain admission for all the Ritsumeikan students into credit-bearing sections of the ASTU courses. For the first 5 years, students with a TOEFL score of less than 550 were segregated into a non–UBC-credit section. For the next 4 years, a greater number of students were mainstreamed under a formula that took their first-term academic performance into account. In academic year 2000–2001, all of the Ritsumeikan students were integrated with their UBC peers in the two ASTU courses, provided that students who had failed to reach a given threshold (on the Wynn Index, which is explained in the next section) got an extra hour of sheltered tutorial instruction.

The Wynn Index

The issue of admissions standards at UBC was raised earlier in this chapter. Like most North American universities, UBC uses a single-number TOEFL score cutoff, 580 for the Faculty of Arts and 570 for Science and Applied Science. (These admissions criteria were current as of 2001. As of spring 2001, alternatives to a single-score cutoff are being actively explored at UBC.) However, it has been very difficult to demonstrate any correlation between TOEFL scores and academic performance at university. The official TOEFL manual, for example, says "correlations between TOEFL scores and grade point averages are often too low to be of any practical significance" (Educational Testing Service, 1992, p. 20). Internal AEP studies have arrived at much the same conclusion. One such study found that correlations between TOEFL scores and course marks from all faculties were extremely low, useful as a predictive device only at the extremes. The study concluded that "other direct and academic-skill-related measures be investigated as alternatives to the indirect measures of proficiency represented by TOEFL" (Berwick & McMichael, 1993, p. 19). Having struggled with this problem in an attempt to maximize AEP students' opportunities to enter the UBC mainstream without throwing them off the deep end before ascertaining whether or not they could swim, an ethically defensible (if mathematically suspect) compromise was struck. The students' first-term averages are added to their highest TOEFL scores to yield a number on a scale that we call the Wynn Index (in honor of its author, Graeme Wynn, the Arts Faculty liaison to the AEP). Students whose Index scores are 600 and above are unconditionally admitted to ASTU 201 and 202 (e.g., a student with a highest TOEFL score of 520 who achieved an 80% first-term average would qualify). Those who fail to reach a 600 Index score are provided with an extra hour of tutorial instruction each week, led by TAs (graduate students) from the Language and Literacy Education Department. Wynn Index scores do not affect placement in second-term LLED courses.

ASTU 201 (Canada, Japan, and the Pacific: Cultural Studies) meets three times a week for an hour, with one additional tutorial hour (plus the additional tutorial hour for Wynn Index underachievers as outlined above), typical of three-credit courses at UBC. The course interweaves Hofstede's (1997) cultural dimensions framework with research in the emerging field of cross-cultural social psychology. The course is distinct in a number of ways. It is team taught on site by faculty from UBC and Ritsumeikan University, and is one of only two courses at UBC (the other being its companion course, ASTU 202) to provide an environment in which a large group of visiting students from Japan shares a classroom with an equal number of students from UBC. Classes are highly interactive, with students expected to reach out across cultures and participate in predictive and ex post facto discussions and problem-solving tasks in class and in tutorials. Students are encouraged to explore their preconceptions about their own and other cultures and share insights with their classmates, TAs, and professors.

ASTU 202 (Canada, Japan, and the Pacific: Political, Economic, and Geographical Perspectives) is cross-listed with Geography 281 in the UBC calendar. This cross-listing is an indication of the progress that the AEP has made in terms of integration with the UBC academic community and represents a major step toward our goal of bringing the AEP and its students further into the UBC mainstream.

ASTU 202 is an introduction to the core political, historical, and geographical forces that shape the Pacific Rim and an exploration of the roles of Japan and Canada in the region. It is similar in structure and intent to ASTU 201, as explained above. The syllabus for ASTU 202 and all of the courses offered under the auspices of the UBC-Ritsumeikan AEP can be accessed online by following the Course Content link at http://www.ritslab.ubc.ca.

LLED 206b and 226b, offered in the second term, retain the format and characteristics of their first-term versions, but their content is more varied, reflecting both the interests of instructors and students. For example, LLED 206b is subdivided into three sections of Language and Language Learning and two sections of Directed Independent Field Research. The sections in Language and Language Learning explore basic topics in the field, including language and graphics organizers, language use, bilingualism, language and the brain, factors in becoming good language learners, and world Englishes. The course seeks to raise students' awareness about what makes a successful L2 learner and how language is represented in the brain. It provides an opportunity to explore the advantages that bilingual and multilingual people have, and introduces students to the field of pragmatics—that vast compendium of knowledge over and above vocabulary and grammar that enables a fluent listener and speaker to function in a language. In addition, problem-solving and critical-thinking skills are fostered through project design and by investigating and solving research problems.

The other two sections of Directed Independent Field Research are open to students who wish to pursue individual research projects. Students submit research proposals, and the topics selected are incorporated into the course's lecture series by the instructor.

LLED 226b is also subdivided, with two sections devoted to Business and Technical Communication, one to Creative Writing, and the remaining two to an Introduction to New Media.

The Business and Technical Communication sections cover several aspects of business communication, including written and oral forms of language. Activities include writing letters, memos, and other business documents; developing marketing projects; creating sales presentation techniques; and learning negotiating skills. A major component of the course is a fundraising competition, in which groups of students set up temporary small businesses (e.g., some students offered cleaning services, others made crafts, some baked cookies) and compete with each other to raise money for a charity of their choice.

The Creative Writing component encourages students to find the writing talent that lies within and to learn to feel free enough to express it. Creative Writing is taught in a workshop format, in that participation is the main emphasis and students learn to write by writing, earning greater fluency in English in the process. Students work mainly with poetry and short fiction forms, but also learn about writing by reading a novel. Activities include short writing projects that are posted and critiqued on an online discussion list, an oral presentation on a choice of published fiction or poetry, a public poetry display, and a final portfolio of self-selected personal writings.

The Introduction to New Media sections invite students to expand their media literacy by exploring and analyzing products of the digital revolution, such as CD-ROMs, Web pages, and digital audio broadcasting, and investigating how these technologies have evolved into new media. The course covers new media history; production, distribution and exhibition in the software business; production, distribution and exhibition in online industries; and the issues and ethics controversy generated by computer-mediated communication. Students research an aspect of new media that interests them and present their findings to the class.

◈ DISTINGUISHING FEATURES

The UBC-Ritsumeikan AEP is distinguished mainly by the fact that it takes a large number of students who would be ineligible to participate in an overseas exchange under normal admissions criteria and provides them with an integrated program of academic credit in content courses, instead of in segregated, non-credit, ESL island courses. The AEP, which won an award for excellence in internationalization from the Association of Universities and Colleges of Canada in 1997, in the category of international student participation, also attempts to provide a comprehensive social and cultural experience for the students through its residential and community outreach components. In addition to its impact on the students, the AEP has had an internationalizing effect on both partner universities and has contributed to a reexamination on UBC's part of the single-score TOEFL criterion for admission to the university.

The AEP is also distinguished by the structure and nature of its curriculum, which was created for the program. The LLED courses were conceived to perform a number of functions. They introduce the students to teaching and learning styles, research methodologies, academic writing requirements, reading workloads, and academic standards of UBC courses. The courses are taught by experienced ESL/EFL teachers, who are able to ease the students' transition by anticipating the difficulties the nonnative-English-speaking students may encounter and structuring the syllabus to facilitate these students' needs, despite the fact that the teachers do not explicitly teach ESL. Course components and assignments are contextualized in terms of how they will contribute to students' learning, helping them to overcome any resistance they might feel to activities that do not fit their schemata of academic environments. Perhaps most importantly, the courses are structured to mirror the students' own experience of studying in a foreign language and adapting to a new cultural environment by immersing them in the adaptation experiences and identity struggles of Canada's immigrant community. This approach permits and encourages students to be introspective about their experiences and examine and discuss them from a variety of perspectives.

The Arts Studies courses are also distinct. They are jointly developed and team taught by faculty from the partner universities. In ASTU 201, the intercultural communication course, faculty attempt to maximize the benefits of having large numbers of students from Canada and Japan in the same classroom by having students sit in mixed groups and engage cross-culturally with the material rather than having them simply sit side by side taking notes.

There are many other features of the program that are not germane to a discussion of mainstreaming students, such as the joint governance model. However, without these underlying structures, it would not have been possible for the model to evolve from a largely segregated, albeit content-based, curriculum, to the present, largely integrated model. The AEP is, in a way, the tip of the iceberg in a growing relationship between the two universities that has broader implications for the internationalization of the institutions and their curricula.

◈ PRACTICAL IDEAS

Get Started

If you wait for ideal terms and conditions before embarking on an innovative program, it will probably never get off the ground. In the beginning, the Ritsumeikan students in the UBC-Ritsumeikan AEP were almost completely academically segregated from their UBC peers. Over the past 10 years, the situation has evolved to where there are no restrictions governing students' integration in AEP courses. We will continue to work to increase access to courses outside the AEP, recognizing that the process is fluid, dynamic, and, above all, incremental.

Aim High

There is no practical reason for ESL students to be kept out of the institutional mainstream. Do not accept received wisdom about what ESL students are or are not capable of, especially if the yardstick is a TOEFL score. Our experience has shown that ESL students whose TOEFL scores are below 500 are capable of achieving success in UBC credit courses. However, such is the power of standardized test scores that some faculty members and administrators will continue to ignore actual results in favor of a TOEFL score.

Give Students Sufficient Contexts for Activities

To reinforce what ESL students have achieved in their course work at UBC, it has been crucial to provide them with sufficient contexts for the work they are asked to undertake. Japanese students' experience of academic environments and the types of activities that are appropriate in those environments are radically different from North American students' experiences. It is not enough to say, "trust us, we know how to provide you with a state-of-the-art program." ESL students must be shown explicitly how their activities fit into the broader educational context in order for them to comfortably undertake, and profit from, those activities.

Work With Individuals Rather Than Departments or Faculties

It is very difficult to move large bureaucracies, but it is relatively easy to engage the interest and cooperation of individual faculty members and administrators. The approach that the UBC-Ritsumeikan AEP has taken is to get individual faculty members to agree to accept students into their classes. Once the students have demonstrated that they can be successful in one context, it is easier to make the next case.

Give Students Opportunities to Become an Asset

Incoming ESL students are too often seen as the only real beneficiaries of their program, aside from the revenue they generate for the host institution. UBC-Ritsumeikan AEP students—the Japanese as well as their UBC residence mates—seek opportunities to contribute. They do obvious things, such as attend campus and community cultural festivals, but they also contribute in ways that reflect more mainstream activities, such as by participating in United Way campaigns (which solicit contributions for charitable organizations) or Shinerama (a Canadian-based organization that raises money to fight cystic fibrosis), or by volunteering in the campus daycare and a preschool program for children with disabilities, among others.

Continue to Innovate

Gaining momentum over time, the UBC-Ritsumeikan AEP was comfortably fulfilling its mandate to provide students from both institutions with an integrated residential and academic program by its 6th year. However, maintaining the status quo often leads to stagnation. AEP students now come with work authorizations, in addition to their student authorizations, to permit them to participate in a variety of community placements, including internships and volunteer opportunities. These outside activities have been incorporated into the curriculum to the benefit of the students and the community. Future plans include offering Ritsumeikan students who are academically strongest an opportunity to stay at UBC for a second year, and a reciprocal international coop program.

◈ CONCLUSION

The UBC-Ritsumeikan Academic Exchange Programme is the first endeavor of its kind in Canada, distinguished by its size and scope. The model has proven successful enough to be copied by UBC in its partnerships with a Korean and a Mexican university, coming on stream this year. The effort to integrate the Ritsumeikan students as completely as possible into the UBC community has brought an international dimension to the UBC campus that would be lost if the Japanese students were secluded in an ESL island program.

Most importantly, the program's curriculum of credit-bearing, content courses open to any student on the UBC campus demonstrates that it is possible to modify admissions criteria creatively without undermining either the academic standards of the host institution or the integrity of the instruction provided to incoming ESL students.

◈ CONTRIBUTOR

Joe Greenholtz holds a BA in psychology from the University of Winnipeg and an MEd in TEFL from Temple University (Japan). He is the executive director of the UBC-Ritsumeikan Academic Exchange Programme and is currently enrolled in a doctoral program in Higher Education Leadership and Policy at the University of British Columbia, in Vancouver, Canada.

◈ APPENDIX

REPRESENTATIVE ENTRY/EXIT PROFICIENCY COMPARISONS FOR THE
UBC-RITSUMEIKAN ACADEMIC EXCHANGE PROGRAMME

Oral Proficiency Scale: 0–5; Writing Proficiency Scale: 1–10

Measure	Entry TOEFL	Exit TOEFL	Entry Interview	Exit Interview	Entry Writing	Exit Writing
Number of students	91	53	98	83	98	78
Minimum score	433	463	1	1+	3.3	5.3
Maximum score	597	597	3	3+	6	9.3
Range	164	134	2	2	2.7	4
Mean	509.8	527.8	1+	2+	0.62	1.3
Variance	777.4	605	0.53	0.38	0.79	1.1
Standard deviation	27.9	24.6	0.73	0.62	0.79	1.15
Median	502	527	1+	2+	4.0	7.3

CHAPTER 10

Preparing Graduate Business Students for Oral Communication in College

Elisabeth Gareis

◈ INTRODUCTION

Oral communication is often neglected in ESOL classes that prepare students for the college mainstream. A recent survey of college-level ESOL programs found that reading and writing courses outnumber listening and speaking courses eight to five; in other words, almost twice as many courses focus on the written word as on oral communication (Gareis, 1999; Institute of International Education, 1997). Reasons for this imbalance include the absence of speech modules in most college entrance exams and the lack of speech requirements for graduation at many colleges. In all likelihood, the traditional predominance of reading/writing assignments and lecture-type classes at the college level also exert a negative influence. There is often little necessity for oral proficiency on the part of students, and college preparation courses reflect this lack of demand.

Unfortunately, this underrepresentation of oral communication in college-level ESOL programs and mainstream classes is in stark contrast to skills needed for workplace success. When employers are asked which skills they value in college graduates, they invariably rank oral communication skills most important (Adler & Towne, 1996; Hagge-Greenberg, 1979; Reinsch & Shelby, 1997; Waner, 1995). Perhaps as a result of workplace requirements, the instructional format of main-stream college classes is beginning to change. One recent trend, for example, is the institution of speaking-intensive curricula at many colleges around the country. These curricula require faculty members to incorporate oral communication tasks into their classes, with the goal of honing students' speech skills for effective communication in the academic context as well as in professional settings (Cronin & Ton, 1991; Jankovich & Powell, 1997; Nicosa, 1997; Schneider, 1999).

Although the shift toward more oral communication is occurring across the curriculum, business schools with employment-oriented majors are especially active in custom-designing courses to prepare students for the realities of the workplace (Cooper, 1997; Knight, 1999; Krugel, 1997; Maes, Weldy, & Icenogle, 1997; Tsui, 1992). Business classes regularly demand fairly high oral proficiency, requiring students to discuss case studies, participate in simulations, complete group work, and give presentations.

◈ CONTEXT

Baruch College is part of the City University of New York (CUNY), in the United States. The College's academic focus is business, and most students have business-related majors in areas such as accountancy, economics, finance, management, and marketing.

In the fall semester of 1998, a total of 14,981 students were enrolled in Baruch College, 1,562 of which were international students, placing Baruch College among the top 25 schools nationwide with the greatest foreign student enrollment (Davis, 1999). Of the 12,386 undergraduate students, 939 (approximately one tenth) were international; of the 2,595 graduate students, 623 (approximately one fourth) were international.

The international graduate students at Baruch College, who are the focus of this chapter, are mostly in their mid- to late 20s. Countries of origin are predominantly located in Asia, with a majority of the students coming from China, Taiwan, India, South Korea, and Japan; other countries with significant contingents include Turkey, Israel, and France. Students are oriented toward employment, with many having previous work experience in their home countries and an increasing number taking elective internship courses while studying at Baruch College. Most graduate business students obtain a Masters in Business Administration (MBA); some receive a Masters of Science (MS). In addition, students may pursue a Doctor of Philosophy (PhD) in business, which is based at Baruch College but granted through the CUNY Graduate Center.

General application materials for the graduate program at Baruch College include the Graduate Record Examination (GRE), the Graduate Management Admission Test (GMAT), and a written statement of purpose. International applicants must also submit results from the Test of English as a Foreign Language (TOEFL) and the Test of Written English (TWE) or the essay rating on the computer-based TOEFL. (The computer-based TOEFL is slowly replacing the paper-based TOEFL and TWE, which will be phased out in the course of the next years. The essay segment on the computer-based TOEFL is identical to the TWE, except that the scoring system is slightly different. The TWE had a scoring system of one to six; the computer-based essay is rated on a scale of zero to six.)

To determine an international student's linguistic preparedness for graduate studies at Baruch College, several factors are considered. The primary indicators of English proficiency are the TOEFL score, the TWE score, the GMAT verbal percentile, and the GMAT analytical writing score. Although no formal minimum requirements exist, a score of 570 on the paper-based TOEFL or a score of 230 on the computer-based TOEFL, a score of 4.5 on the TWE, a GMAT verbal percentile of 35, and a GMAT analytical writing score of 4.0 are seen as guidelines. If one or more of the scores fall below these levels but some exceed them, secondary indicators of English proficiency are taken into account. These indicators include the student's application essay, résumé, and letters of recommendation, as well as opportunities the applicant has had to use written and spoken English.

Although students with the minimal scores listed above may be admitted to Baruch College MBA or MS programs, their transition into the mainstream was problematic in the past. Not possessing strong skills in listening, speaking, reading, and/or writing, the students could not adequately participate in the many communication-oriented activities of their business classes.

Over the years, business faculty complained that a large percentage of their international graduate students had problems with the communication tasks required for successful completion of classroom and out-of-class assignments. Following these complaints, the administration decided to aid students in need of assistance and to create a course that would prepare them for the linguistic and cultural requirements of the mainstream.

◈ DESCRIPTION

In the fall of 1997, representatives of the Business School at Baruch College contacted Continuing Studies, the English Department, and the Department of Communication Studies with a request for a coordinated course sequence for international graduate students with low English language proficiency. The course sequence was created in the following year and has been taught since 1998.

Placement in the course sequence is determined by a combination of test scores. Guideline minimum scores to avoid the requirement are 610 on the TOEFL, 5.0 on the TWE, a 45 GMAT verbal percentile, and a 4.5 GMAT analytical writing score. These cut-off points result in an enrollment of approximately one third of all incoming international graduate students.

The course sequence consists of a presemester, full-time immersion program, a course in written communication, and a course in oral communication. The immersion program, entitled Advanced Business English for International MBA and MS Students, is offered through Continuing Studies, lasts 1 month, and is taken before the student's first mainstream semester. It focuses on general language skills as well as on business English and includes an oral review (e.g., dialogues, drills, and idiomatic integrations), accent reduction, intensive reading and writing, a lecture series, and field trips. The immersion program lays the groundwork for the courses in written and oral communication, which are taught through the departments of English and Communication Studies during the first mainstream semester and concentrate on the skills needed for academic success. It is the latter course in oral communication that is the focus of this case study.

To determine the exact mainstream needs in oral communication, a faculty survey was administered. The survey resulted in the following list of concerns, which are addressed under Practical Ideas:

- general comprehensibility (especially pronunciation, fluency, and vocabulary)
- class participation
- negotiating misunderstandings
- effective interaction during small-group work
- information retrieval in research settings
- familiarity with U.S. cultural patterns (especially as they pertain to initial student adjustment and communication issues)

- discussion participation
- familiarity with U.S. educational culture (e.g., classroom etiquette, faculty expectations, internships, and issues affecting international students)
- group presentations
- individual presentations

Based on the survey results, we created a course entitled Spoken English for International Students (COM 8191). The course is offered in multiple sections, with an average of six sections per semester and a maximum number of 15 students per section. Classes are 75 minutes long and meet once a week, for 14 weeks. Currently, three teachers teach the sections. The curriculum described in this case study serves as a model; all topics should be covered in the course of the semester, but teachers are free to replace individual activities if they wish. Although students receive credit for the course (1½ credit hours) and must pass it in order to graduate, grades are not included in the students' grade point average.

Many colleges offer courses that prepare ESOL students or accompany them into the mainstream. A common obstacle in the design and administration of these mainstreaming courses is the limit on contact time. This problem also exists for the Spoken English for International Students course. The short duration of the course (75 minutes per week for one 14-week semester) required the inclusion of the following elements to aid student progress: (a) efficient use of limited class time, (b) availability of a fully equipped language lab, (c) assistance of tutors for pronunciation training, and (d) curricular revisions based on student evaluations and teacher recommendations.

Academic communication skills take a long time to develop. A course of only one semester is therefore suited, at most, to introducing the skills to students, confirming their understanding of the subject matter, and allowing them to practice the techniques briefly under the supervision of a teacher. Because the most efficient use of class time is for supervised practice, it was decided that students should complete a great deal of work outside of class. Thus, all topics in Spoken English for International Students are prepared through homework assignments that include language lab work, interviews, group work, and readings. Class time is used for a brief review of the material, followed by an intensive practice period and time for reflection. Students are made aware that each oral communication skill covered in class has the spotlight for only one class session and that they should continue practicing the skills beyond that session. In addition to preparatory work, efficiency is attempted by combining skills activities with cultural or linguistic content. When students practice group presentation techniques, for example, they do so by sharing their research findings on U.S. educational culture, thus acquiring oral communication skills and content at the same time.

Due to the limited class time and the oral communication focus of the course, instruction would not be possible without a well-equipped language lab used for the preparation and practice of lessons. The Baruch College language lab is a computerized lab with over 30 audio, video, and software programs. Multiple materials are available for all covered topics so that students can select what is most helpful and interesting to them. After completing assignments, students hand in written summaries and reactions to their selections, and the teacher responds with written comments and feedback.

Another invaluable resource in the course is the availability of tutors to assist students with pronunciation problems. Two tutors, both adjunct professors with backgrounds in accent reduction and speech training, were hired through the college's academic support system. These tutors met with individual students by appointment. The tutors are a necessity because the curriculum focuses on academic communication skills and does not permit exclusive or even extensive attention on pronunciation. Whereas language lab work and brief weekly pronunciation practice in class are sufficient for some students, others need additional assistance. One-on-one tutoring has proven to be most effective for this purpose.

The original curriculum of Spoken English for International Students was based on faculty concerns. In the 2 years since the inception of the course, several elements have been revised to address needs expressed by the students. Thus, more videos have been purchased for the language lab, some assignments have been replaced, and the public speaking section has been expanded due to popular demand. In the future, a segment on business meetings may be added and possibly one on interviewing skills (perhaps at the loss or reduction of the library treasure hunt and the picture description exercise, which can easily be shortened or covered gradually throughout the semester). The instructors teaching the course also initiate curricular revisions. They then either incorporate these changes into their individual classes or into the whole curriculum to serve as a model for all instructional staff members.

◈ DISTINGUISHING FEATURES

The course activity that invariably receives the highest score on end-of-semester course evaluations is the public speaking segment. A great majority of students have had no exposure to public speaking training in their home countries; yet their academic and future workplace environments are replete with informal as well as formal public speaking requirements. Mainstreaming programs should therefore consider making a public speaking segment part of their curricula, especially if they focus on employment-oriented majors.

Maybe the most important ingredient for success in oral communication courses is the time available for supervised practice (i.e., practice that is observed by a teacher so that the students can receive feedback, repeat rehearsals, and effectively reflect on the experience). In Spoken English for International Students, sufficient contact time is ensured by small class sizes and the requirement that students prepare for each session prior to class time. One feature that would provide additional assistance is more frequent or longer class meetings. Considering the students' full schedules, however, the desire for more frequent or longer classes will be difficult to fulfill.

A shortcoming in Spoken English for International Students is the fact that students are placed in the course on the basis of non-speaking test scores: None of the entrance exams (e.g., the TOEFL, the TWE, the GRE, or the GMAT) contains speech modules. Unfortunately, the correlation between written and oral proficiency is moderate at best (Henning & Cascallar, 1992; Isonio & Cooperman, 1992); students with adequate writing skills may not have adequate oral proficiency and vice versa. As a result, students are sometimes placed in the course even though they have adequate oral proficiency, and, by the same token, students who need the course are exempted from it due to their sufficient writing test scores. The course could therefore be improved through more appropriate placement assessment.

Alternatives include testing prior to admission in the form of the internationally administered Test of Spoken English (TSE) or a locally administered placement exam after the students' arrival. The issue is under discussion at Baruch College, and a change may be effected soon. Programs considering the creation of an oral communication course for ESOL students should weigh assessment options carefully and include pre- and posttesting measures.

Scheduling and Grading

In a 14-week semester, one session each is devoted to the following topics: introduction and diagnostic speech test, pronunciation overview, conversation management, continuing story exercise, library treasure hunt results, picture description, student-facilitated discussion on U.S. cultural patterns, student-facilitated discussion on nonverbal communication, group presentations on U.S. educational culture, group presentations on public speaking techniques (videotaped), discussion of videotaped group presentation and practice of audiovisual equipment use, final presentations (two sessions), and final exam. Besides the listed topics, each class session includes a pronunciation segment consisting of a quiz and practice period on selected pronunciation features.

Grades are a composite of class participation (10%), lab attendance and homework assignments (20%), quizzes (20%), final presentation (20%), and final exam (30%). All in-class activities and out-of-class assignments are evaluated for completeness and oral proficiency (including overall comprehensibility, accuracy, and fluency). To receive a passing grade, students must have a C average or better at the end of the semester.

◈ PRACTICAL IDEAS

The Spoken English for International Students course follows a task-based syllabus, designed to provide instruction and practice in all areas singled out by the surveyed faculty. The following is a description of how each faculty concern is addressed through course activities. Although the following activities are tailored to the needs of Baruch College students, the underlying needs are quite common among international students. The activities should therefore be readily applicable to other educational contexts.

Stress General Comprehensibility

Pronunciation

At the beginning of the semester, a diagnostic test is administered in the language lab to determine the students' articulatory proficiency and fluency levels. Based on the results of the diagnostic test, each student is given a list of pronunciation items to practice in the language lab and with speech tutors. For example, a student having difficulty differentiating between /r/ and /l/ is asked to complete all exercises available in the lab focusing on these sounds. If necessary, students are referred to a tutor for individual work on sound or intonation problems. In addition, some class time is spent each week on selected pronunciation features. To prepare for these lessons, students read a pronunciation text and listen to the accompanying materials in the language lab (Dauer, 1993). Student progress is monitored through weekly (oral) quizzes and ongoing, informal evaluations during class.

Fluency

Fluency issues are addressed throughout the semester in a variety of interactive, impromptu exercises and rehearsed speech presentations. Most prominently, students keep an audiotape journal on which they record at least 15 minutes of uninterrupted speech each week. Tape journal topics are chosen by the students and range from informal accounts of weekend excursions to rehearsals for a mainstream class presentation. The teacher selects one or two random tapes per week, listens to the students' work, and responds by recording feedback and comments directly on the tapes.

Vocabulary

As is the case with pronunciation and fluency, vocabulary development is an ongoing process and the subtopic of many activities. One class session is devoted solely to questions of vocabulary, however. In preparation for this session, students listen to a number of language lab materials on idioms as a homework assignment, noting their 10 favorite expressions. During the class session, techniques for vocabulary development are discussed and a *continuing story* exercise is conducted. After the students explain their idiomatic expressions, the teacher begins telling a story, and, one by one, students continue it, using each other's (but not their own) expressions. The exercise sensitizes students to the need for using new words in written and oral communication to make them part of their active vocabulary.

Facilitate Class Participation

Class participation in the form of student questions and contributions to discussions is not important or even desirable in some cultures. To introduce the topic, U.S. standards for classroom participation are discussed and compared with standards in the students' home countries. Throughout the semester, students are asked to participate actively in the course and practice standard U.S. behaviors. The teacher keeps track of student contributions (number and length) during each class session and provides tips for improvements to passive students after class. Once during the semester, students are also asked to record themselves in one of their mainstream classes—with the knowledge of their professor—as they ask a question or contribute to a class discussion. The recording is shared with the teacher, who supplies comments on the recordings with feedback and advice.

Help Students to Negotiate Misunderstandings

In day-to-day interactions, nonnative speakers often avoid the negotiation of meaning and act as if they understood, even if another person's utterance was not, or was only partially, clear. Numerous opportunities for learning are thus wasted, and frequent misunderstandings ensue. From the beginning of the semester, the teacher checks students' comprehension (of the teacher and each other) and ensures that students negotiate meaning whenever they have problems understanding or making themselves understood. To negotiate misunderstandings, students are asked to follow a number of steps. Listeners who have difficulty understanding should ask for repetition first, then for slower speech, followed by a request for the spelling of the problematic word, and, finally, for a paraphrase or explanation. Speakers who have difficulty making themselves understood should first repeat the sentence or word in question with more careful enunciation and special attention to stress and rhythm, then paraphrase or explain it, and, finally, write it down for the listener. Although these clarification techniques are used throughout the semester, one class session is set aside for their concentrated practice. During this session, students have to describe a picture to their classmates, who try to follow the instructions and draw the visual. Whenever comprehension is impeded, listeners as well as speakers use the step approach to negotiate meaning and clarify the issues at hand.

Train Students in Effective Interaction During Small-Group Work

Business students often have to complete small-group assignments in their main-stream classes. The groups frequently meet outside of class and function on an informal level. Good conversation management skills are needed for effective participation. Students get introduced to conversation management skills in the language lab through audio materials on functions and notions (Jones & von Baeyer, 1983; McClure, 1996) and a video series on conversational styles (Steinbach, 1996). They are asked to note general information (e.g., about turn-taking behavior and cultural differences) as well as expressions for a variety of conversation management strategies (e.g., starting a conversation, giving feedback, hesitating, interrupting, preventing interruptions, and closing a conversation). In the following class session, small groups of three to four students are recorded conducting impromptu conversations in which they use as many of the studied conversation management behaviors and expressions as possible. After the session, students listen to the recordings of their conversations and analyze their performance with the help of self-evaluation forms that inquire about their use of covered strategies, such as the number and length of turns, the use of fillers, and the use of conversation management expressions. The teacher provides feedback on the students' analyses of their conversations.

Practice Information Retrieval in Research Settings

To practice research skills, students are sent on a library treasure hunt that requires spoken interaction with library personnel. Before students embark on their journey, the class discusses techniques for polite inquiry. Students then use these techniques to ask library staff members a variety of questions (e.g., the location of microfilms and microfiches, interlibrary loan policies, check-out procedures, use of research software). Students then share their findings during the next class session.

Inculcate Familiarity With U.S. Cultural Patterns

The course examines U.S. cultural patterns, especially those pertaining to initial adjustment and communication issues, through a variety of readings. Topics include U.S. friendship patterns, table etiquette, taboos, and nonverbal communication (Althen, 1988; Wanning, 1997). Students read the assigned selections at home and discuss them in class, using the procedures discussed in the next section.

Encourage Discussion Participation

Instructors usually agree that the best way to learn is to teach. By the same token, students who are quiet during class discussions may learn to participate by having to facilitate a discussion once themselves. Two class sessions are used for the practice of effective discussion gatekeeping and participation techniques (Hill, 1982). Students form small groups and take turns facilitating discussions on previously assigned readings. The gatekeepers prepare discussion questions, listen carefully to their group members, keep the discussion on track, ensure equal participation, and summarize contributions at the end. Group members are asked to participate actively, refrain from dominating or withdrawing, and remain interculturally sensitive.

Increase Familiarity With U.S. Educational Culture

To learn about U.S. educational culture, students gather information on a variety of topics, including classroom etiquette, faculty expectations, internships, and issues affecting international students. They conduct their research as a homework assignment through interviews with mainstream students, professors, and administrators as well as through readings (Levine & Adelman, 1982; Skillman & McMahill, 1996). During the next class session, they discuss their findings in small groups, with the goal of presenting them to the whole class in the form of one of the three group presentation techniques described in the following section.

Teach Group Presentation Skills

Students study three techniques for presenting group findings:

1. final report
2. panel discussion
3. symposium

To practice the techniques, the class is divided into three groups, each sharing their previously assigned research on U.S. educational culture. After about 15–20 minutes, each group presents its findings, using one of the three group presentation techniques. The final report group selects one spokesperson to present the group's results; the panel discussion group discusses its issue in front of the whole class; and the symposium group members take turns speaking about different aspects of the topic. After the group presentations, the whole class discusses the advantages and disadvantages of each technique.

Give Guidelines for Individual Presentations

Guidelines for public speaking can be found in many textbooks and self-help manuals. A compilation of such guidelines is used in the course to introduce public speaking techniques to students who, to a great extent, have had neither training nor experience in public speaking (Gareis, 1998). The reading material is divided into three to four parts and assigned to small groups. Each group is responsible for covering its selection and presenting a summary to the whole group during the next class session. The guidelines include information on preparing and delivering speeches, the use of audiovisual aids, communication anxiety, and different types of speeches. Students are videotaped and later analyze their performance with the help of self-evaluation forms. The presentations thus allow students to learn (from each other) about public speaking techniques and to practice public speaking at the same time. The results of the students' self-evaluations are discussed during the next class, with special attention given to their use of audiovisual aids. The following two class sessions are reserved for the semester's final presentations. Students select topics related to their majors and give 5-minute speeches, which are graded according to adherence to the covered public speaking principles.

Even though students are evaluated on their work throughout the semester, the end-of-semester assessment tools—the final presentation and a final exam—carry the most weight. The final exam is a SPEAK Test, which is the institutional version of the TSE (Educational Testing Service, 1996).

◈ CONCLUSION

A course such as Spoken English for International Students is well suited for helping students enter the mainstream in communication-intensive majors. Through its focus on oral communication skills and culture, the course prepares students not only for effective participation in college-level classes but also for interaction on interpersonal levels and integration into the college community, which has proven instrumental in the experience of academic success (Kapoor & Smith, 1978). More importantly perhaps, the course provides a bridge between college and workplace. With employers consistently ranking oral communication skills highest among skills desired of college graduates, students are often underprepared for the demands in the workplace. The course lays a foundation in oral communication upon which students can build throughout their studies. By the time they graduate, students' initial investment of time will have paid off, and they will be more likely to compete successfully in an increasingly English-speaking marketplace—whether they remain in the United States or return home.

◈ CONTRIBUTOR

Elisabeth Gareis is associate professor in the Department of Communication Studies at Baruch College–CUNY, in the United States. She teaches ESOL, public speaking, intercultural communication, and international business communication, and serves as ESOL coordinator in the Department of Communication Studies. She is also coauthor of the textbook series *A Novel Approach* (on the use of literature and film adaptations in the ESOL classroom; University of Michigan Press) and has been editor of the NYS TESOL publication *Idiom*.

CHAPTER 11

From ESL Into the Mainstream: Assessing Student Outcomes

Mark Patkowski

⬦ INTRODUCTION

This case describes a 3-year period in the life of a college-based, credit-granting, ESL program whose mission is to prepare ESL students to function successfully in the academic mainstream of the college. The period in question, 1994–1997, was one of major change and intensive self-examination. During this time, the ESL program at Brooklyn College and its faculty found a new home in the English department, thoroughly revamped its curricular offerings, and embarked upon a systematic process of monitoring the program's success in promoting students' transition into the mainstream.

The chapter begins with an overview of the current trend toward outcomes assessment (OA) in higher education throughout the United States and continues with a brief description of the restructuring of the ESL program at Brooklyn College. The central focus, however, is on presenting a case study in implementing a process of OA, largely based on the use of existing program and institutional information. Finally, 10 practical suggestions are offered to ESL professionals who are interested in experimenting with their own approaches to evaluating the effectiveness of their programs.

⬦ CONTEXT

The Broader Context: The OA Movement in U.S. Higher Education

As a comprehensive review of performance reporting in higher education (New York State Education Department, 1996) demonstrates, OA has been a subject of much interest in academic circles, state legislatures, and at the federal level since the 1980s. Traditional input indicators, such as faculty credentials or the size of library holdings, have increasingly been replaced by indicators of outputs or outcomes. An early call for OA came in 1986 from the National Governors' Association, which urged colleges "to implement systematic reforms that use multiple measures to assess undergraduate student learning. The information gained from assessment should be used to evaluate institutional and program quality" (New York State Education Department, 1996, p. 3).

The federal Student-Right-to-Know and Campus Security Act, passed in 1990, mandated the nationwide reporting of graduation and transfer rates, and professional and accreditation organizations, such as the American Association for Higher Education (1992), the American Association of State Colleges and Universities ("States Mount Retention Effort," 1994), and the Commission on Higher Education of the Middle States Association of Colleges and Schools (1994, 1996) all began to emphasize OA requirements.

In New York, the Regents Commission on Higher Education made performance assessment a key component of the 1996–2004 plan for higher education in the state (reported in New York State Department of Education, 1996) and, in a highly critical examination of the City University of New York (CUNY), a Mayoral Advisory Task Force repeatedly called for outcome-based accountability: "No CUNY institution or program should be supported if it does not provide clear, objective information about the quality and productivity of its efforts" (Schmidt et al., 1999, p. 101).

Yet political pressures ought not to be the primary driving force behind the decision to carry out OA programs. There are sound educational reasons for colleges, departments, and programs, including ESL programs, to engage in OA activities:

> As an integral part of teaching and learning, assessment promotes self-reflection and evidence-based thinking about teaching, learning, and student growth. Not only can it lead to improvement in both the quality and quantity of learning by students, it also responds to their needs for personal development. Therefore, faculty can apply assessment findings to improve student learning in the classroom and throughout the curriculum as a whole. (Commission on Higher Education of the Middle States Association of Colleges and Schools, 1996, p. 9)

However, what exactly is OA and how is it done? Fortunately, as one noted OA expert observes, "assessment activities don't need a rocket scientist to be implemented" (Nichols, 1995, p. 32). For Nichols, the three key requirements are:

1. identifying a limited set of specific goals ("intended educational outcomes," p. 10) to be achieved; Nichols recommends limiting the number of goal statements to three to five.

2. selecting appropriate assessment practices; carefully considering existing means and resources. As Nichols writes, "The perfect means of assessment will never exist; however, choices will need to be made and implemented based upon the department's judgment of the best means available at the time" (p. 32).

3. "closing the loop" (p. 53) by using OA results to improve instructional programming. To quote Nichols again, "The end product of virtually all assessment activities (except some accountability initiatives) is the improvement of academic programming based upon the use of assessment results. Without being able to demonstrate such use of assessment results, all previous activities fall short of their intended purpose" (p. 53).

The Local Context: The Forces That Led to Implementing OA in a College ESL Program

The 1980s and 1990s witnessed unprecedented emigration to the New York metropolitan area, and, by 1993, more than 45% of CUNY's entering students were foreign born (City University of New York, 1994). At Brooklyn College, ESL enrollment doubled during the 1980s. Simultaneously, severe budgetary constraints were causing a significant decline in the number and morale of full-time ESL faculty, and ESL adjunct instructional costs were greatly increasing, to the irritation of other departments. These feelings came to a head in 1991, when a college task force declared the ESL program both expensive and educationally inefficient.

As a result, the program was transferred to the English department in 1994 with a mandate for reform. The ESL faculty identified several areas in need of change and selected four key goals:

1. to develop integrated reading and writing skills courses

2. to develop linked courses in collaboration with faculty in other departments

3. to restructure the program so as to prevent students from getting stuck in a cycle of failure and repetition of advanced-level ESL reading and writing courses

4. to develop an ESL Learning Center that could provide effective, individualized instruction and assistance to students

In addition, it became clear, even though none of the participants was currently familiar with OA literature, that systematic procedures would be needed to monitor the effectiveness of the new program. A plan to gather statistical data was drawn up, and a faculty member was given responsibility for program evaluation and research.

◈ DESCRIPTION

During the 1994–1995 academic year, the traditional ESL courses, which were divided into levels of proficiency and language skills (reading, writing, speaking), continued to be offered while a plan for curricular reform, based on the principles of *integration* and *intensification*, was being formulated.

The first principle was reflected in new integrated skills courses (reading-writing-speech courses at the lower levels, and reading-writing courses at the higher levels), and in greater emphasis on offering a *blocked* program of linked ESL and content classes (the ESL Block Program), in conjunction with the college's Freshman Year Block Program. The faculty felt that curricular integration reflected the best current thinking in L2 instruction and in retention practices (see, e.g., Benesch, 1988; Brinton, Snow, & Wesche, 1989; Chamot, & O'Malley, 1987; Cochran, 1992; Crandall, 1992; Gaies, 1991; Snow, Met, & Genesee, 1989; Tinto, Love, & Russo, 1993, 1994) and would promote the students' transition to the mainstream.

The second principle, that of intensification, was put into practice by creating special repeater classes for students with multiple failures in advanced ESL writing, and by establishing a new ESL Learning Center. The repeater classes featured reduced enrollment (10–12 students) and a workshop approach with peer tutoring and laboratory resources. The ESL Learning Center provided individual and small-group instruction, using undergraduate tutors (half of whom were former ESL students) trained by the center's director. The course structure of the new ESL program is illustrated in Table 1 of the Appendix.

In the fall of 1995, the restructured program was implemented, with 809 students from more than 20 language backgrounds enrolled in 51 sections. The overwhelming majority of the students were U.S. residents (rather than foreign nationals with student visas). About two thirds had graduated from high schools abroad and most of the rest from New York schools. Additional demographic data are presented later in this chapter.

Upon entering college, all students took the CUNY basic skills tests in reading (the Reading Assessment Test, or RAT), writing (the Writing Assessment Test, or WAT), and math. The WAT gave students the choice of two topics and 50 minutes in which to write an essay that was scored holistically by two trained raters, whereas the RAT was a multiple-choice test of reading comprehension developed by the College Board. Passage of the tests was deemed to certify minimal readiness for the academic demands of college courses. Students who did not pass and who were nonnative speakers of English were assigned to the ESL program. Movement within the program was based upon end-of-semester placement tests in reading and writing. Students in upper level classes had to retake and pass the WAT and the RAT to exit the program and enter the mainstream. The WAT and RAT thus represented a textbook case of high-stakes testing with all the consequent pressures on both students and teachers. (These instruments, which had been in place since 1978, have since been discontinued by the university, only to be replaced with an essentially similar pair of high-stakes tests.)

With the new structures in place, data collection began in earnest, with the Fall 1994 data (representing the "traditional" program) used as a baseline.

◈ DISTINGUISHING FEATURES

This section describes three distinctive types of OA activities that were carried out over the 3-year period:

1. examining student outcomes within the ESL program
2. examining student outcomes in the mainstream
3. carrying out surveys to examine specific issues

Each activity is discussed in terms of the three steps described by Nichols (1995): setting goals, implementing appropriate means of assessment, and closing the loop by acting upon the results.

For each type of OA activity, the first two steps are presented in figure form. A discussion of the third step, closing the loop, follows.

Examining Student Outcomes Within the ESL Program

Steps 1 and 2

Through the analysis of existing data (e.g., class rosters, grade rosters, WAT and RAT result lists) routinely collected by the ESL program, it was possible to ascertain whether several important program goals were being met. Three examples are given in Figure 1.

Step 3: Closing the Loop

Although the principles of integration and intensification that had guided the curricular reform process appeared to be quite promising in the area of writing, the

Step 1: Goals	Step 2: Assessment
1. Increase pass rates on basic skills tests	Clear improvement on writing test (from 28% in Fall 1994 to 55.7% in Fall 1997), but the reading pass rate remains within the 65–79% band, with no clear upward or downward trend.
2. Compare effectiveness of instructional approaches	Pass rates on writing test are higher for linked ESL-content courses and for intensified repeater writing courses than for traditional skills-based ESL courses (see Table 2 in Appendix). Reading results are more ambiguous.
3. Evaluate effects of increased ESL and content faculty collaboration on student outcomes in ESL courses	Grant makes possible series of workshops to enhance faculty collaboration in the Spring 1997 ESL Block Program (17 faculty members from 6 departments and 175 students are involved). Comparison with Spring 1996 program shows moderate increase in program exit rate—proportion of ESL students mainstreamed—and significant increase in level exit rate—proportion of students passing on to the next ESL level (see Table 3 in Appendix).

FIGURE 1. Examining Student Outcomes Within the ESL Program: Three Examples

reading results suggested the need for a closer look. Plans for further investigation were developed (see Figure 3).

Because faculty collaboration did appear to have a positive effect upon educational outcomes, as shown in Example 3 in Figure 1 (see, also, Example 1 in Figure 2), it was recommended to the college administration that it create sufficient lead-up time to allow instructors the opportunity to confer with their colleagues about texts, syllabi, and general collaboration, and to set dates for regular meetings during the course of the semester. It was further recommended that some form of remuneration, especially for adjuncts, be given because of the extra time and work involved. The administration responded by appointing a Faculty Fellow to help coordinate the Freshman Block program and to foster faculty interaction; however, the suggestion concerning remuneration was not acted upon.

Examining Student Outcomes in the Mainstream

Steps 1 and 2

By accessing the college registrar's computer-based student records, it was possible to examine the academic transcripts of current and past ESL students and thus to monitor their performance in the mainstream. Three examples of mainstream outcome studies are given in Figure 2.

Step 3: Closing the Loop

The recommendations made to the administration based upon the improved outcomes from enhanced faculty collaboration were already discussed in the preceding section.

Step 1: Goals	Step 2: Assessment
1. Evaluate effects of increased ESL and content faculty collaboration on outcomes in content courses	Comparison of grades in content courses of ESL Freshman Year Block Program for the Spring 1996 and 1997 semesters shows overall pattern of gentle improvement, with increases in four out of five comparisons (see Table 4 in Appendix).
2. Verify the appropriateness of linking lower level ESL courses with content courses	Average grades in five content courses in Spring 1996 and 1997 Freshman Year Block Program are compared for students at different ESL levels through Analysis of Variance (ANOVA). Students enrolled at the lowest levels (ESL 11 and 12 data were merged due to low enrollment in ESL 11) perform poorly, never reaching the 2.0 grade point average (GPA) required for maintenance of matriculation and graduation. Students at intermediate and advanced levels obtain satisfactory grades (see Table 5 in Appendix).
3. Assess the long-term academic performance of former ESL students in the mainstream	Three-year follow-up study with Spring 1997 cohort classifies students as "enrolled and successful," "enrolled but unsuccessful," or "no longer enrolled" on basis of retention, pass rates in freshman composition, GPA, credit accumulation, completion ratio of attempted credits, and performance in college's core courses. Earlier 3-year cohort study (Patkowski, 1991) of Fall 1985 cohort in traditional ESL Program provides accessible, if slightly dated, comparison. Only the 127 entering students in 1997 cohort are included, to match 1985 cohort. Results after 3 years are clearly better for the 1997 cohort, with higher retention rates (see Table 6 in Appendix) and a higher rate of academic success (see Table 7 in Appendix).

FIGURE 2. Examining Student Outcomes in the Mainstream: Three Examples

The findings from Example 2 in Figure 2 and the results of a student survey (Example 3 in Figure 3) engendered a further recommendation to the administration that the courses that make up a block should be conceptually meaningful and appropriate to the language proficiency level of ESL students. Due to a 1996 mandate by the CUNY Board of Trustees placing a 15-month limit on the completion of ESL requirements at senior CUNY colleges, the two lowest levels of ESL instruction were eliminated as of Fall 1998, rendering moot the issue of linking low-level ESL courses. However, the remaining ESL blocks have been restructured to consist of a core of three basic courses: an integrated ESL course, a language support course (e.g., Vocabulary Building or Speech), and a mainstream, content course.

The findings from Example 3 in Figure 2 supported the notion that linking integrated ESL courses in a well-planned block program does appear to promote more effective mainstreaming of ESL students in the long run.

Carrying Out Surveys to Examine Special Issues

Steps 1 and 2

From time to time, we found it useful to develop relatively simple questionnaires to investigate issues that arose from the types of analysis described above (or through other circumstances). Three projects are described in Figure 3.

Step 1: Goals	Step 2: Assessment
1. Examine the perceptions of the ESL faculty about the functioning of the restructured program	Faculty questionnaire is developed that solicits responses to statements on rating scale (quantitative data) as well as open-ended written responses (qualitative data). Good participation rate, with 36 of 38 questionnaires returned. Results reveal basic approval for restructured program. However, there is a perception that reading instruction has suffered.
2. Gather basic demographic and educational background data	Student questionnaire is developed and distributed to all students in the block program in Spring 1997. Results include • average age: 22 years • age range: 17–41 years • average time in United States: 3 years (maximum 18 years) • high school: 32% finished in United States • no prior higher education: 65% • most common first languages: Russian, Chinese, Spanish, and Creole • language other than English most spoken at home: 97% • married: 15.5% • with children: only 9.3% • working: 40% • hours worked per week: 4–70 (average: 24 hours)
3. Compare students' perceptions of the ESL and mainstream block programs	Questionnaire for ESL block students is developed, based upon earlier survey of mainstream block students (J. Bernstein, 1996). Mostly quantitative data (responses to statements on rating scales) are elicited. Results indicate less satisfaction among ESL than mainstream students: • 54% (vs. 73%) rate the program as good or very good • 64% (vs. 83%) are prepared to recommend or strongly recommend the program to a friend • 51% (vs. 68%) agree or strongly agree that the program makes college life easier • 50% (vs. 52%) agree or strongly agree that the contents of Block courses are presented in an interrelated manner

FIGURE 3. Carrying Out Surveys to Examine Special Issues: Three Examples

Step 3: Closing the Loop

After the results from the faculty survey were considered in conjunction with the results on the reading test from Figure 1, it was decided to reintroduce a stand-alone ESL reading course into the curriculum and to extend the intermediate reading-writing course by 1 instructional hour per week.

The results of the demographic student survey showed that, surprisingly, the majority of the ESL students were fairly traditional: young, single, recently out of high school, and either not working or working part time. At the same time, more than a third of the students did not fit this traditional mold.

An updating of the demographic and educational data every 2 years or so was deemed advisable, to allow the program to track changes in the composition of its student body. As recent turmoil in CUNY's admissions policies has severely affected ESL enrollment, these surveys have, in fact, proven quite valuable in documenting this impact. The results of the student opinion survey, as stated in the discussion of Example 2 in Figure 2, led to the recommendation to the administration that the courses that make up a block be made more conceptually meaningful.

◈ PRACTICAL IDEAS

Here are some general guidelines you could use to introduce OA into your ESL program and evaluate its effectiveness in promoting transition into the mainstream. Once OA has been introduced, new issues specific to your own situation will doubtlessly arise; these will be answered through your own discussions, both within your program and institution and with outside sources, and your own search through the literature.

Inform Yourself

Two publications that have been quoted frequently in this chapter (Commission on Higher Education of the Middle States Association of Colleges and Schools, 1994; Nichols, 1995) are eminently readable handbooks for the beginning practitioner, as are Banta, Lund, Black, and Oblander (1996) and Erwin (1991). A recent report of interest is Schilling and Schilling (1998). An excellent online resource is "Internet Resources for Higher Education Outcomes Assessment" (n.d.) This site contains dozens of links to discussion groups, forums, archives, assessment-related pages of colleges and universities, and more; it is a veritable OA treasure chest. There is also an ERIC Clearinghouse on Assessment and Evaluation site (http://ericae.net/).

Try to Engage As Many Members of the Faculty and Administration As Possible

The literature agrees: Any process of OA, to be successful, must reflect the professional judgment of a majority of the faculty in a program or department. Additionally, there must exist a partnership between the faculty and the administration. One approach might be for a small group of faculty to begin developing an assessment plan at the classroom level and to seek, gradually, to engage more and more colleagues in the program or institution. On the other hand, under certain circumstances, such as those described herein, when a program is engaged in major curricular restructuring, it may be possible to move more quickly. The goal—to engage as many members of the faculty and staff—is clear. The means will depend on local conditions.

Do Not Be Afraid of the Big Bad Wolves: Testing and Statistics

The key to good OA practice is developing clear educational objectives and making use of results to improve instruction and learning. The assessment activities can be kept at a relatively simple level, and so can the statistics. If no one can understand the assessment procedures or the analysis of the results, little of use will emerge. Besides, there is bound to be a colleague or two who are interested in such matters; get them involved.

Set Clear and Limited Objectives

Getting a group of faculty members to achieve consensus on most matters can be a task of Herculean proportions. Limit the number of objectives. Think of three to five concrete goals to be achieved by the students upon completion of your program. Seek to identify the strengths and weaknesses of your program. The key characteristic of objectives is that they be ascertainable; think of your statements of educational objectives as testable hypotheses. You need not restrict yourself to identifying specific sets of skills or bodies of knowledge that students need to learn; you might consider growth in students' personal and affective development, too (e.g., comfort in L2 use).

Select Practical Means of Assessment

Carefully examine the data you already have at your disposal. What questions can be answered with existing information? Much useful information is already available: institutional registration and transcript data, student evaluations of faculty, alumni surveys, program attendance, and grade rosters. Construct your own assessment materials, such as questionnaires, sparingly; such efforts can be very time consuming as well as duplicative of existing materials.

Select Multiple Means of Assessment

Use more than one type of measure. Consider qualitative approaches (e.g., interviews, portfolio reviews) as well as quantitative ones (e.g., standardized tests). You may wish to include cognitive and attitudinal assessment; the latter might include not only student attitudes but, for instance, the attitude of content professors toward ESL students.

Establish a Time Line

Be realistic. Most of us do not work without deadlines. Therefore, specify an implementation time line.

Establish Clear Responsibility (and Rewards) for Carrying Out the Assessment

Responsibility for data collection and analysis must be assigned to a specific person or persons. Ideally, said person or persons should receive appropriate recognition;

depending on local factors, this might take the form of a title, instructional release time, or extra remuneration.

Close the Loop

Assessment is carried out to meet the needs of internal and external audiences. Internally, within the program or institution, as repeatedly stressed, the primary purpose of OA activities is to promote greater instructional effectiveness. For external audiences, the program should be able to demonstrate that it is meeting its objectives. OA reports cannot simply be filed away in dusty drawers. Results must be communicated effectively, and action must follow the written word.

Learn By Doing

In the words of a well-known marketing advertisement, "Just do it!" This is the best way to learn.

◈ CONCLUSION

College ESL students can and do succeed in the mainstream; indeed, several studies have shown that they compare quite favorably to their non-ESL peers in terms of academic outcomes (e.g., see Abraham, 1993; Benesch & Block, 1995; Bers, 1994; Isonio, 1994; Patkowski, Fox, & Smodlaka, 1997). However, in the current political context, the need to document these successes is more urgent than ever. Besides, and more importantly, it makes good educational sense to engage in OA in order to improve instructional programming and to promote better teaching and learning. And do not forget:

> Assessment activities don't need a rocket scientist to be implemented. They do need careful review of the assessment options (means) available and consideration of the statements of intended student outcomes and resources available (usually small), as well as the specific requirements placed upon the department. (Nichols, 1995, p. 32)

◈ CONTRIBUTOR

Mark Patkowski is an associate professor in the English Department of Brooklyn College–CUNY, in the United States, where he teaches undergraduate and graduate ESL, English, and Liberal Studies courses. He served for several years as assistant to the ESL program director, with special responsibility for data collection and analysis, and served on the College Committee on Outcomes Assessment during the Middle States reaccreditation process. In addition, he has served as chair of the College Basic Skills Committee and as cochair of the Writing Across the Curriculum Committee. He has also obtained grants and published in the area of assessment and evaluation.

◈ APPENDIX

TABLE 1. STRUCTURE OF NEW ESL PROGRAM

Course	Content	Hours Per Week	Credits
ESL 11	Beginning reading-writing-speech (integrated course)	9 + 1 lab hour	0
ESL 12	Low intermediate reading-writing-speech (integrated course)	9 + 1 lab hour	1
ESL 14	High intermediate reading-writing (integrated course)	6 + 1 lab hour	2
ESL 14.1	High intermediate writing (stand-alone course)	4 + 1 lab hour	2
ESL 15	Advanced reading-writing (integrated course)	6 + 1 lab hour	3
ESL 15.1	Advanced writing (stand-alone course)	4 + 1 lab hour	2
ESL 15.2	Repeater writing (intensified course)	2 + 3 hours of tutoring	2
ESL 0.03	Reading workshop (intensified course)	2 hours	0
ESL 1.5	Intermediate speech (stand-alone course)	3 hours	1

TABLE 2. WAT OUTCOMES UNDER VARYING INSTRUCTIONAL CONDITIONS

Course Type (semester)	WAT Pass Rate	N
Traditional advanced writing course (Fall 1994)	27.8%	212
Linked ESL-content courses in Freshman Year Block Program (Fall 1994 and Spring 1995)	47.5%	99
Intensified repeater writing (Spring and Fall 1995)	48.0%	148
New stand-alone advanced writing (Fall 1995)	34.5%	174
New integrated advanced reading-writing (Fall 1995)	31.3%	131

TABLE 3. WAT SUCCESS RATES IN SPRING 1996 AND SPRING 1997

	N	Spring 1996	Spring 1997	df	Chi Square	P
Program exit rate (WAT=8 for all)	157	29.4%	34.1%	1	0.33	ns
Level exit rate (WAT=6 in ESL 14 and 8 in ESL 15)	157	52.9%	70.8%	1	1.77	.028

TABLE 4. MEAN GRADES IN CONTENT COURSES IN SPRING 1996 AND SPRING 1997

Course	N	Spring 1996 mean grade	Spring 1997 mean grade	df	t	P
TVR 6.5	112	1.61	1.65	110	0.16	ns
FILM 1	68	1.50	2.41	66	−2.52	.007
ECO 0.1	61	2.09	2.46	59	−1.24	ns
CORE 2.1	49	2.24	3.06	47	−2.26	.014
CORE 1.1	51	3.05	2.58	49	1.14	ns

TABLE 5. TWO-WAY ANOVA ON MEAN GRADES IN FIVE CONTENT COURSES

Semester	ESL Level		
	ESL 11-12	ESL 14	ESL 15
Spring 1996	1.60 (n=49)	2.26 (n=28)	2.64 (n=19)
Spring 1997	1.73 (n=61)	2.55 (n=37)	2.71 (n=15)
Source of Variation	df	mean square	F	p
Semester	1	4.27	2.81	ns
ESL level	2	23.90	15.71	.000
Interaction	2	0.21	.14	ns
Within groups	239	1.52		

TABLE 6. RETENTION RATES FOR ENTERING COHORTS IN THE TRADITIONAL ESL PROGRAM AND THE ESL BLOCK PROGRAM

Semester	Traditional Program		Block Program	
	N	Retention Rate (%)	N	Retention Rate (%)
1st	271	100	127	100
2nd	239	88.2	107	84.3
3rd	198	73.1	93	73.2
4th	165	60.9	76	59.8
5th	127	46.9	70	55.1
6th	108	39.9	66	52.0

TABLE 7. ACADEMIC SUCCESS AFTER 3 YEARS FOR ENTERING COHORTS IN THE TRADITIONAL ESL PROGRAM AND THE ESL BLOCK PROGRAM

Academic Success Rating	Traditional Program		Block Program	
	N	%	N	%
Not currently enrolled	153	56.5	61	48.0
Enrolled ("unsuccessful")	53	19.6	16	12.6
Enrolled ("successful")	65	24.0	50	39.4

CHAPTER 12

ESL Students in the Mainstream: Teacher Expectation and Learner Need

Effie Papatzikou Cochran

✦ INTRODUCTION

However sound it may be pedagogically, mainstreaming—like any challenging endeavor—is not without attendant difficulties. The moment when ESL students realize that the rest of their academic careers will really depend upon the skill with which they comprehend and manipulate a foreign language probably occurs on the first day of their first mainstream class, and it has to be one of the most traumatic moments they will ever experience. Few of us can understand how difficult it is to function successfully in an institution whose lifeblood is a language one has not yet mastered.

An incongruity between ESL students and their new mainstream teachers usually compounds the students' trauma. Few non-ESL-trained teachers have had the education and experience to understand nonnative students' distinctive difficulties, and some may even feel they should not be asked to be knowledgeable about them—perhaps on the grounds that they involve developmental, even allegedly remedial, skills for which regular teachers should not be held responsible.

It was predicted that by the beginning of the 21st century, more than 50% of entering City University of New York (CUNY) freshmen would come from homes in which some other language besides English is spoken (CUNY, 1995). Because this prediction has now come true (oral communication, CUNY central admissions office), concern for mainstreamed ESL students' academic well-being can no longer be labeled merely a minority issue at CUNY.

✦ CONTEXT

In the early 1980s, when my interest in mainstreaming began, there were not many published studies on the subject. However, with public opinion currently against free access to higher education, reassessing all previous assessments seems to be the norm. Consequently, some structured studies of the attitudes and expectations of mainstream faculty in interaction with mainstreamed ESL students have begun to appear. Studies on student academic needs are still few because these students have no political clout. Most of them have no voting rights and, hence, no advocates. Because states view them as financial burdens, ESL students' needs are last on the list of what drives urban universities, including CUNY, where fiscal issues, especially laws like the welfare laws, drive their policies.

Researchers on the subject of mainstreaming have taken a variety of approaches and produced as many outcomes. To name some, Ostler (1980) surveyed 131 ESL students at the University of Southern California and asked them to assess their own academic skills and needs. Although students felt comfortable in social and business settings, they evidenced discomfort with complex academic material. In the Johns (1981) survey of 200 San Diego University faculty (various disciplines), it was discovered that students' *receptive* skills (listening and reading) were weaker than their *productive* ones (speaking and writing), suggesting that ESL teaching priorities had been out of balance. Horowitz (1986) took a different approach by analyzing the teacher handouts and assignments of 38 Western Illinois University faculty in order to advise teachers of English for academic purposes (EAP) and mainstream faculty. Mason (1995) surveyed 18 faculty and 26 international graduate students at Georgetown University and noted a growing appreciation of the necessity for oral/aural skills. Mason found in particular that "the difficulty of lecture comprehension increased when [an instructor's] lecture style required the oral participation of foreign graduate students and their aural comprehension of other students' speech" (p. 205).

A more recent in-depth study on attitudes is the Youngs and Youngs, Jr. (2001) study, both descriptive and explanatory in nature. It is a report on a survey of 143 junior high/middle school mainstream teachers in the midwest United States and offers constructive suggestions after exploring teachers' attitudes toward ESL students on the basis of five predictors:

1. general educational experiences
2. ESL training
3. contact with diverse cultures
4. prior contact with ESL students
5. demographic characteristics

The results show that the more cultural exposure to diverse cultures teachers have—either via traveling, studying a foreign language, or receiving ESL training and multicultural education courses—the more likely it is that mainstream teachers' positive attitude toward cultural diversity will be enhanced. Therefore, mainstream teachers' attitudes do indeed have a positive or negative effect on ESL students' learning. Finally, Russikoff (1996) questioned 392 faculty in various disciplines at California State Polytechnic University, in Pomona; surveyed their practices vis-à-vis their ESL students; and collected her respondents' comments. These included such remarks as "Grammar, spelling, punctuation, vocabulary, forgiven for ESLs"; "I emphasize and grade content equally"; and "I give them many more chances to revise and come to the office."

If only the first two of Russikoff's findings are typical, then the academy is currently a long way from consensus on how to teach ESL students in the mainstream. Indeed, do mainstream faculty hold mainstreamed ESL students to the same standards that they require for native speakers, or do they adjust their standards for ESL students? Do they disregard or overlook grammatical mistakes in writing or mispronunciation errors in speech, or do they judge them more harshly? Do they lower their standards for all students? How do ESL students react? Are they encouraged or intimidated by their new environment? Do they blossom or shrink under mainstream tutelage? How might the efforts of the ESL student and the mainstream teacher be brought into a more harmonious, more productive, closer academic relationship? My pilot project endeavored to clarify these issues by means of a questionnaire that was distributed to my John Jay College colleagues (see Appendix).

The Pilot Study

Because of present reservations about ESL support and the concern that the removal of so-called remediation courses from all the 4-year colleges of CUNY has created, disquiet over mainstreamed ESL students' academic progress has increased. Therefore, ESL practitioners feel that it is imperative for non-ESL-trained teachers in the mainstream to share the responsibility of helping ESL students in their courses.

Exploring how to help ESL students and their mainstream teachers converge onto a mutually intelligible and supportive pedagogical path is the point of this piece of research-in-progress. Reported here are the preliminary results of a pilot survey of faculty experience with mainstreamed ESL students. More precisely, my research sought to find out what mainstream teachers do or do not do to help ESL students in their classes. I also hoped that their answers would reveal their hidden attitudes toward language minority students in general.

❖ DESCRIPTION

With the help of a Professional Staff Congress-City University of New York grant (PSC-CUNY), I conducted this pilot study at my college (see Appendix), where our two levels of ESL courses have sociology and criminology content. A pilot survey was sent in mid-April 1998 to mainstream faculty in 14 departments of the John Jay College of Criminal Justice in CUNY. The departments were Anthropology, African-American Studies, Art/Music/Philosophy, English, Government, History, Law and Police Science, Mathematics, Psychology, Public Management/Fire Science/Public Administration, Sociology, Speech and Theatre, Science, and Thematic Studies. The number of surveys sent to each department was four, with the exception of Government and Public Administration, which were sent five each, and Sociology and English, which were sent six and seven respectively due to the large number of faculty.

The departments of Foreign Languages, Puerto Rican Studies, and "Search for Education and Elevation of Knowledge" (SEEK), which are already supportive of ESL students, were not included in the study.

The in-house pilot had a good response and revealed interesting data. It has also been helpful for the revision of the survey for future use.

The Questionnaire

The survey questions were designed so that they would elicit mainstream faculty expectations of and attitudes toward ESL students in their courses. They were inspired by Russikoff's (1996) convention presentation, "What Content Faculty Really Expect of ESL Writers."

I created the pilot questionnaire itself after consulting several surveys and requesting input from colleagues in our field and from my college's and university's offices of Institutional Research and Analysis. I sent out 63 questionnaires to John Jay colleagues and received 43 responses.

The questions covered four broad categories, requiring short answers or ranking checks, for which tables are provided. There were also three open-ended questions, the responses to which are discussed in detail but not presented in table form because it would have been impossible to tabulate so many single answers.

◈ DISTINGUISHING FEATURES

In Category A, I chose to correlate the survey questions with the results and some interpretive analysis to demonstrate the degree to which content teachers participate in the second language acquisition process.

Treatment of Mistakes in Papers and Exams of Nonnative English Speakers

Question: In your course, when you grade papers or exams of nonnative English students, do you forgive or ignore mistakes in:

1. Content: content, detailed development, topic identification, factual support, original ideas?

The possibilities to check off were: *always, often, sometimes,* and *never* for all Category A questions (see Table 1).

In each of these content areas, a majority of professors chose never to forgive or ignore content and content-related mistakes by ESL students. However, the range of relative importance given to the specified content-related areas is interesting. The highest percentage (71%) chose "content" as the most indispensable feature of an acceptable ESL paper, while a low of 53% picked "detailed development" as indispensable. The remaining three areas—topic identification, factual support, original ideas—clumped close together in the middle (64%, 62%, 62% respectively) between the two extremes.

Clearly, while most mainstream professors are unwilling to forgive mistakes of content where ESL students are concerned, many more are willing to tolerate poor

TABLE 1. FORGIVE OR IGNORE MISTAKES IN CONTENT WHILE GRADING PAPERS OF NONNATIVE ENGLISH STUDENTS

Content	Total N	Always/Often N	%	Sometimes N	%	Never N	%
Content	42	1	(2)	11	(26)	30	(71)
Detailed development	43	2	(5)	18	(42)	23	(53)
Topic identification	42	1	(2)	14	(33)	27	(64)
Factual support	40	1	(3)	14	(35)	25	(62)
Original ideas	40	1	(3)	14	(35)	25	(62)

TABLE 2. FORGIVE OR IGNORE MISTAKES IN ORGANIZATION WHILE GRADING PAPERS OF NONNATIVE ENGLISH STUDENTS

Organization	Total N	Always/Often N	%	Sometimes N	%	Never N	%
Organization	42	2	(5)	18	(43)	22	(52)
Cohesion	43	2	(5)	20	(47)	21	(49)
Clarity	43	4	(9)	21	(49)	18	(42)
Sequencing	43	4	(9)	19	(44)	20	(47)
Sufficient length	42	49	(10)	17	(40)	21	(50)

skills related to writing (detailed development). The other areas fall in the middle because they appear to be connected to both content and writing skills.

2. Organization: organization, cohesion, clarity, sequencing, sufficient length?

At least half of the respondents indicated that they would never forgive or ignore mistakes in organization (52%) or sufficient length (50%), but a considerable number of them also admitted that they sometimes forgive mistakes in cohesion (47%) and clarity (49%). This is clear evidence that the majority of these teachers are understanding of the nonnative linguistic status of their ESL students (see Table 2).

In this context, it is also useful to see the *always/often* and *sometimes* columns together: In this organization area, almost as many professors *always/often* or *sometimes* do forgive ESL errors as those who *never* do.

3. Editing, audience, vocabulary: appropriate word, editing, audience awareness, writer's purpose, and register?

Professors were even more lenient when it came to ESL students' use of the appropriate word or term. A clear majority (60%) said they sometimes ignored vocabulary and terminology confusion, whereas only a minority (19%) insisted that they never ignore such inaccuracies. Table 3 also documents a continuing shift toward tolerance of linguistic errors when the first five tables are viewed in sequence.

TABLE 3. FORGIVE OR IGNORE MISTAKES IN EDITING, AUDIENCE, AND VOCABULARY WHILE GRADING PAPERS OF NONNATIVE ENGLISH STUDENTS

Editing, Audience, Vocabulary	Total N	Always N	%	Often N	%	Sometimes N	%	Never N	%
Appropriate word	43	3	(7)	6	(14)	26	(60)	8	(19)
Editing	41	1	(2)	4	(10)	17	(41)	19	(46)
Audience awareness	37	1	(3)	2	(5)	17	(46)	17	(46)
Writer's purpose	40	1	(2)	19	(48)	20	(50)		
Register	37	1	(3)	6	(16)	20	(54)	10	(27)

TABLE 4. FORGIVE OR IGNORE MISTAKES IN LANGUAGE USE WHILE GRADING PAPERS
OF NONNATIVE ENGLISH STUDENTS

Language Use	Total N	Always N	%	Often N	%	Sometimes N	%	Never N	%
Subject/verb agreement	43	4	(9)	5	(12)	18	(42)	16	(37)
Sentence construction	43	4	(9)	6	(14)	25	(58)	8	(19)
Preposition and article usage	43	4	(9)	7	(16)	21	(49)	11	(26)
Verb parts/ tense usage	43	4	(9)	5	(12)	20	(47)	14	(33)
Idioms	43	5	(12)	9	(21)	23	(53)	6	(14)

4. Language use: subject/verb agreement, sentence construction, preposition and article usage, verb parts/tense usage, and idioms?

According to Table 4, the majority of mainstream professors said that they forgive mistakes in all areas of language usage, at least *sometimes* or *often/always*. As expected, the lowest percentage of teachers (14%) said they never forgive mistakes in the use of idioms, which are among the hardest language tools to master, especially in English.

This subcategory continues to show respondents demonstrating notable lenience about language use difficulties.

5. Mechanics: capitalization, punctuation, spelling, format/paragraphing, and legibility?

In the subcategory of mechanics, mainstream teachers seemed to be more understanding and flexible as far as spelling, punctuation, and even paragraphing were concerned. The exception was the "legibility" entry, where professors marked students more harshly. Of respondents, 53% declared that they never forgive illegible papers, which indicated great frustration in deciphering students' handwriting, perhaps especially those whose native languages do not have Latin-based characters (see Table 5).

TABLE 5. FORGIVE OR IGNORE MISTAKES IN MECHANICS USE WHILE GRADING PAPERS
OF NONNATIVE ENGLISH STUDENTS

Mechanics	Total N	Always N	%	Often N	%	Sometimes N	%	Never N	%
Capitalization	43	6	(14)	5	(12)	17	(40)	15	(35)
Punctuation	43	6	(14)	5	(12)	18	(42)	14	(33)
Spelling	43	5	(12)	6	(14)	19	(44)	13	(30)
Format/paragraphing	43	6	(14)	4	(9)	18	(42)	15	(35)
Legibility	43	6	(14)	3	(7)	11	(26)	23	(53)

Tables 1–5 show a clear progression of increasing forgiveness or lenience as the subcategories move from content, through mixed subject understanding/writing skills, to more exclusively literary techniques. This progression is characteristic of increasing majorities of the professors polled, and it is probably the most objective or least opinion-biased of the results produced by the questionnaire. In Categories B, C, D, E, F, and G, however, professors' individual opinions become more prominent.

Major Study Skills and Their Relation to Course Success

Category B is designed to ascertain instructors' analysis of the importance of the four skills to academic success.

Question: Which of the following major skills are most essential to success in your courses?

A high percentage (98%—the highest in the survey) of professors declared reading to be the single most essential skill for success in their courses, with writing coming in a close second (93%). Listening was ranked distant third (70%), while speaking trailed behind the others (42%) (see Table 6).

Hidden within the 98% are a complex of skills given that *reading,* like *detailed development* in Category A, Subcategory 1, is not precisely defined (i.e., Does reading mean speed reading, comprehension, ability to manipulate information, profundity?) The dominance of reading and writing is somewhat surprising, in view of the enormous importance of oral/aural skills in the workplace, not to speak of professors' anecdotal complaints about their students' oral unintelligibility and incomprehension. This result may be more a reflection of the professors' own education than a reflection of their view of what their students' priorities should be.

Rigor in Grading Native and Nonnative Speakers of English

Category C is designed to ascertain instructors' perceptions of how equitable their behavior is with native and nonnative students.

Question: Do you grade ESL students and native speakers of English with equal rigor (or laxity) in the following areas?

Table 7 incorporates two distinct areas of grading: skills (summary writing, critical thinking, and interpretation/analysis) and assignments (the other items in the table). It is interesting that the "skills" received the three highest yes votes (75%, 92%, 73%), perhaps because the professors correctly saw skills as applicable to all assignments.

TABLE 6. RANK ORDER OF THE MOST ESSENTIAL SKILL FOR SUCCESS IN COURSES (N=43)

Skills	Rank Order	N	%
Reading	1	42	(98)
Writing	2	40	(93)
Listening	3	30	(70)
Speaking	4	18	(42)

TABLE 7. GRADING ESL STUDENTS AND NATIVE ENGLISH SPEAKERS
WITH EQUAL RIGOR OR LAXITY

Grading Aspects	Total N	Yes N	%	No N	%	N/A N	%
Summary writing skills	36	27	(75)	4	(11)	5	(14)
Critical thinking skills	37	34	(92)	2	(5)	1	(3)
Personal response/reaction papers	35	20	(57)	4	(11)	11	(31)
Interpretive skills/analysis of author's work	37	27	(73)	5	(14)	5	(14)
Short critiques	36	25	(69)	3	(8)	8	(22)
Oral presentations/reports	26	16	(62)	5	(19)	5	(19)

In response to whether professors graded ESL and native English speakers with equal rigor, the negative responses in grading critical thinking are considerably lower (5%) than the positive ones (92%). This certainly indicates that professors try to grade all students (native and nonnative speakers) alike, regardless of their linguistic background.

However, a number of respondents refused to answer this comparative question. For instance, although the grading of oral presentations or reports was not applicable to some courses (19%), quite a few responses to this particular entry were missing without qualification. Again, although for some (14%) summary writing skills were not necessary for their course, some professors chose not to respond here. A similar pattern was the case with reaction papers.

General Practices Toward ESL Students in Mainstream Courses

In Category D, the survey attempted to detect professors' general practices and attitudes toward ESL students in their mainstream courses.

Question: When you have language minority students in your class, do you (see statements in Table 8):

As Table 8 shows, quite a few responses were missing when it came to relaxing standards for ESL students, as well as for lowering standards for all students. The encouraging thing is that mainstream professors do not relax standards for ESL students (85%) or lower standards for all students (97%)—or if they do, they do not admit it. It is also very encouraging that faculty see ESL students for individual conferences more often (62%) than native speakers, and offer them more personal attention. However, there is a split in giving ESL students more chances to revise papers (49% yes to 51% no). As is well known, multiple drafts and revisions are a guarantee of writing improvement.

Attitudes Toward Mainstreaming and Mainstreamed ESL Students

The following three categories (E, F, G) were open-ended questions, the answers to which shed considerable light on attitudes toward mainstreaming and mainstreamed

TABLE 8. GENERAL PRACTICES WITH ESL STUDENTS IN REGULAR CLASSES

Statements	Total N	Yes N	%	No N	%
Relax standards for ESL students	34	5	(15)	29	(85)
Lower standards for all students	36	1	(3)	35	(97)
Place equal emphasis on content and mechanics when grading papers	38	21	(55)	17	(45)
Give ESL students more chances to revise	41	20	(49)	21	(51)
See ESL students more often in one-to-one conferences	39	24	(62)	15	(38)

ESL students. It should be noted, however, that—due to the open-ended and individualized nature of these questions—no tables were constructed, and only the highlights are reported below.

Question: If you had a CHOICE, would you accept language minority (ESL) students in your courses? Why or why not? Explain. (E)

This open-ended question of Category E concerned the acceptance of language minority students (see Appendix). Respondents generally showed tolerance and inclusiveness; 39 out of 43 showed positive attitudes toward John Jay ESL students, although some qualified their responses, requiring ESL students to meet certain conditions such as:

- equal competence with non-ESL students working at college level
- need for exposure to and contact with native English speakers to practice their language skills
- need for basic standards to be met (grammar and simple English)
- need to identify themselves as ESL students (without indicating the reasons why)

Among the more positive comments on this question were

- Yes, because they often know more of literature than my native speakers.
- Many of our ESL students are brighter than the "native majority" ones.
- ESL students bring a unique exposure to otherwise monolingual classes.
- In most cases [their] written English is the same quality as that of native speakers.
- There is no difference between native speakers and ESL students.

And a constant, sympathetic mantra was

- more resources are needed for ESL students.

Difficulties With ESL Students

This section gauges the instructors' perception of difficulties in their experiences with ESL students.

Question: List difficulties you have had with ESL students. (F)

With the exception of 7 out of 43 respondents who did not offer an opinion, the majority generally agreed with the following list of difficulties with ESL students:

- ESL students are shy and reluctant to speak in class but often speak in their native language during class.

- Because of their limited English vocabulary, they struggle with texts and lectures, memorizing buzzwords and using prefabricated phrases without understanding.

- They use nonstandard English and do not speak clearly.

- They do not take advantage of one-to-one conferences with faculty or of college resources.

- ESL students have difficulty with grammar, spelling, and sentence construction and demonstrate an inability to think critically.

Mainstream faculty again seem to want nonnative speakers to identify themselves as ESL students. The students' course load was also cited as a difficulty, but at the same time faculty observed that ESL students seem to have many of the same difficulties that native speakers do.

Recommendations for ESL Students in the College Mainstream

This section elicits information on how instructors guide students through the mainstreaming process.

Question: What recommendations can you make for ESL students in the college mainstream? (G)

Again, 7 respondents out of 43 did not comment in this section. Variations on the recommendations listed below appeared in many surveys. The most frequently repeated recommendations were "identify themselves as ESL students," "reduce course load," and "speak only English."

- Learn to speak clearly, read more newspapers, magazines, and books in English.

- Make friends and form study groups with native speakers.

- Practice English speaking, reading aloud, and writing more.

- Take advantage of the writing/ESL center, other resources, and enroll in tutorial classes.

- Don't be afraid to speak up; communication with professors is important; precise communication in jobs is required.

It should be noted that many respondents again remarked that the difficulties they had with ESL students were the same as those they had with native speakers. This is possibly a reflection of CUNY's inner city, older, working, student population. But the fact that many professors want ESL students to identify themselves is a double-edged sword. For professors who are sympathetic to nonnative speakers, it works to the students' advantage to identify themselves as ESL students. On the other hand, ESL students may be automatically penalized because of a professor's preconceptions that such students do not belong in college before they have perfected (or at least standardized) their English skills and have acquired nearly flawless academic English.

Some professors are unaware that it takes a long time for a person raised in another cultural and linguistic environment to convert into the anglophone, linear way of thinking and writing (Kaplan, 1966). In fact, some older adults are never able to master the English exposition of an argument perfectly. For some cultures, it is even impossible to criticize anybody or anything, and that makes it twice as difficult for them to learn to practice critical thinking, especially when—in many cultures— students are only required to memorize and regurgitate text. Hence, patience and understanding are required on the part of mainstream faculty.

The plea for more resources indicates sympathetic attitudes toward ESL students. Professors' disparaging comments about course overloads are valid. However, what is reflected here is ESL students' need to acquire the English language faster while being enrolled in mainstream courses and interacting with native speakers. Enrollment in mainstream courses also enables language minority students to finish their college requirements at the same time because their financial sources dry up after a certain number of years. Obviously, they cannot afford to spend all their grant money on "developmental" English alone.

Regular joint ESL/mainstream faculty development sessions that will take consciousness raising into consideration as well as deal with practical issues are highly desirable. Workshops that place teachers in their students' shoes have always been successful.

❖ PRACTICAL IDEAS

I hope that readers will be able to use my questionnaire to help them develop their own. When planning your own survey, you may want to consider the following steps.

Use "Soft," Nontechnical Terms

A few respondents were confused by my use of the technical term *register* in Question A.3.e (see Table 3 and Appendix). Respondents can give you better responses when they fully understand what you are asking them, so finding nontechnical synonyms is useful.

Define Terms for Respondents

Under *skills* in Question B (see Table 6), one respondent asked that the question about reading be more precisely phrased, with *reading* needing a definition (e.g., does it refer to reading comprehension or some other aspect of that skill?). In other words, it helps to anticipate the kinds of questions your respondents might have about your terms.

Organize Items of the Same Kind Together

One respondent asked that I move interpretive skills/analysis to the position directly under critical thinking in Question B (see Table 7) so that the three skills would be together, followed by the three assignments. Organizing your questions into related sets helps respondents make conceptual links.

Involve Students as Respondents Also

Studies like this will remain one-sided until ESL/EFL students themselves are enabled to voice their needs and expectations. If possible, consider also videotaping a linguistically varied, representative group of students who would answer candidly questions about their difficulties in the mainstream.

In general, with all the talk about the changing face of America's color, and the need for computer experts and other cyberspace workers to be imported from abroad, it behooves us to continue to pay attention to the educational needs of the immigrant population that is already here.

◈ CONCLUSION

In general, it has been encouraging to see that John Jay College faculty think highly of their ESL students, acknowledging that they work hard and "some have been very good, even among my best students." It is also wonderful to see professors spend time with ESL students, encouraging, advising, and referring them to the resource and writing centers to get help. Both faculty and administration also acknowledge the fact that, usually, the salutatorian and valedictorian who speak at graduation at John Jay (and at other CUNY campuses) are nonnative speakers of English who started their college careers with ESL courses.

But despite the encouragement and the accolades that are bestowed on language minority students, there is presently a strong desire on the part of some CUNY professors, administrators, and especially some CUNY trustees to prohibit such students from entering college unless they are college ready. This feeling may stem from the long-standing, widespread frustration with the large numbers of underprepared native-English-speaking students (possibly the products of our disintegrating public school system) entering freshman classes. In fact, some of these so-called native English speakers do hear or speak another language or dialect at home, and many are literate in neither language (see Cochran, 1998–1999). It seems likely that this frustration would be extended to those ESL students with strong accents and different cultural backgrounds, some of whom also lack more sophisticated English language skills.

As I concluded at the end of my introduction to the CUNY handbook,

> These are challenging times for CUNY. The diversity of our students presents us with a golden opportunity to integrate their rich linguistic and cultural backgrounds into our classes. Multi-culturalism is an asset, not a liability, a fact to which most urban educators bear ready witness. Because of the presence of ESL students, classes are richer and more complex, albeit more demanding . . . A challenge, to be sure, but most assuredly not a negative one. (1992, p. 3)

◈ ACKNOWLEDGMENTS

I am grateful for the guidance of John Jay–CUNY statisticians Gail Hauss, Mary Nampiaparampil, and David Crook. I appreciate the constant support of Anastasia Raptis, P. J. Gibson, and Provost Basil Wilson. Finally, I owe a debt of gratitude to my cooperative John Jay colleagues, who took the time to respond to my survey, and for my PSC-CUNY grant, without which this study would not have been possible.

◈ CONTRIBUTOR

Effie Papatzikou Cochran is an associate professor in the Department of English at John Jay College of Criminal Justice of the City University of New York. She is a teacher educator, author of numerous articles, and editor of the 1992 CUNY handbook, *Into the Academic Mainstream: Guidelines for Teaching Language Minority Students.* Her article on Greek diglossia appeared in *International Journal for the Sociology of Language* in 1997. She is coeditor of *Issues in Gender, Language Learning, and Classroom Pedagogy* (2001), commissioned and published by NJTESOL-NJBE in collaboration with Bastos Educational Publications.

◈ APPENDIX: PILOT QUESTIONNAIRE FOR MAINSTREAM FACULTY

CUNY College_____ Department _____

Rank _____ Male_____ Female_____

Number of years teaching college _____ F/T_____ P/T_____

Names and Level(s) of Courses you teach _____

_____

_____

Please answer the following questions as they pertain to the categories below:

A. In your course, when you grade papers or exams of nonnative English students:

Do you forgive or ignore mistakes in (check appropriate boxes):

	Always 1	Often 2	Sometimes 3	Never 4
1. CONTENT				
a. content_____				
b. detailed development _____				
c. topic identification_____				
d. factual support _____				
e. original ideas _____				

	Always 1	Often 2	Sometimes 3	Never 4
2. ORGANIZATION				
a. organization				
b. cohesion				
c. clarity				
d. sequencing				
e. sufficient length				
3. EDITING, AUDIENCE, VOCABULARY				
a. appropriate word/term				
b. editing/proofreading				
c. audience awareness				
d. writer's purpose				
e. register (e.g. formal vs. informal)				
4. LANGUAGE USE				
a. subject/verb agreement				
b. sentence construction				
c. prep. & article usage				
d. verb parts/tense usage				
e. idioms				
5. MECHANICS				
a. capitalization				
b. punctuation				
c. spelling				
d. format/paragraphing				
e. legibility				

B. Which of the following major skills are most essential to success in your courses? (Please check as many as apply.)

_____ reading (of texts)

_____ writing (of reports/papers)

_____ speaking (oral reports, discussions)

_____ listening (to lectures, audio/video, panelists)

C. Do you grade ESL students and native speakers of English with equal rigor (or laxity) in the following areas? (Please answer YES, NO, or N/A.)

a. summary writing skills

b. critical thinking skills

c. personal response/reaction papers

d. interpretive skills/analysis of author's work

e. short critiques

f. oral presentations/reports

D. In general, when you have language minority students in your class (please answer YES or NO),

a. Do you relax your standards for ESL students?

b. Do you lower your standards for all students in that class?

c. Do you put equal emphasis on content and mechanics when you grade their papers?

d. Do you give ESL students more chances to revise?

e. Do you see ESL students more often in one-to-one conferences?

E. If you had a CHOICE, would you accept language minority (ESL) students in your courses? Why or why not? Explain.

_____

_____

_____

_____

F. List difficulties you have had with ESL students:

_____

_____

_____

_____

G. What recommendations can you make for ESL students in the college mainstream?

_____

_____

_____

_____

Please use the remainder of this page for additional comments. Thank you for taking the time to respond and for being candid. Your answers will help both our ESL or language minority students and our faculty who teach them in the college mainstream.

Effie P. Cochran

Effie Papatzikou Cochran
Associate Professor, English Department
John Jay College of Criminal Justice

References

Abraham, P. (1993). Reading proficiency and academic success: Assessment and prediction for native and nonnative speakers of English. *Dissertation Abstracts International, 54*(05), Section A, 1741.

Accelerated Reader (Version 5.12) [Computer software]. (2000). Wisconsin Rapids, WI: Renaissance Learning.

Adler, R. B., & Towne, N. (1996). *Looking out/looking in: Interpersonal communication* (8th ed.). New York: Harcourt Brace College Publishers.

Aird, E., & Lippmann, D. (Eds.). (1983). *English is their right: Strategies for teachers in the multilingual classroom.* Melbourne, Australia: AE Press.

Althen, G. (1988). *American ways: A guide for foreigners in the United States.* Yarmouth, ME: Intercultural Press.

American Association for Higher Education. (1992). *Principles of good practice for assessing student learning.* Washington, DC: Author.

Arkoudis, S. (1995). *Clash of cultures: Mainstream teachers' working knowledge and English as a second language (ESL) pedagogy.* Unpublished MEd minor thesis, University of Melbourne, Melbourne, Australia.

Arkoudis, S. (2000). *The epistemological authority of an ESL teacher in science education.* Unpublished doctoral dissertation. University of Melbourne, Melbourne, Australia.

Banta, T., Lund, J., Black, K., & Oblander, F. (1996). *Assessment in practice: Putting principles to work on college campuses.* San Francisco, CA: Jossey-Bass.

Barnett, J. (1999). *Review of ESL provisions in South Australian Catholic schools.* Adelaide, Australia: South Australian Commission for Catholic Schools.

Barnett, J., Walsh, J., Pangyres, M., & Hender, N. (1998). *Review of the English as a second language (ESL) program.* Adelaide, Australia: Department of Education, Training and Employment.

Benesch, S. (Ed.). (1988). *Ending remediation: Linking ESL and content in higher education.* Washington, DC: TESOL.

Benesch, S., & Block, E. (1995). The cost of public education. *College ESL, 5*(1), 47–51.

Bernstein, B. (1996). *Pedagogy, symbolic control and identity.* London: Taylor & Francis.

Bernstein, J. (1996). The Brooklyn College block program: Student experience and satisfaction. In *Transformations: Working papers from an interdisciplinary seminar on the Freshman Year experience* (pp. 7–24). New York: Office of the Dean of Undergraduate Studies, Brooklyn College, City University of New York.

Bers, T. (1994). English proficiency, course patterns, and academic achievements of limited-English-proficient community college students. *Research in Higher Education, 35*(2), 209–234.

Berwick, R., & McMichael, W. (1993). Findings related to course marks, proficiency test results and student questionnaires for the 1992–1993 LANE-Ritsumeikan programme. Vancouver, Canada: University of British Columbia Department of Language Education.

Board of Studies. (1995). *The curriculum and standards framework*. Melbourne, Australia: Author.

Board of Studies. (1996). *The ESL companion to the English curriculum and standards framework*. Melbourne, Australia: Author.

Board of Studies. (1997). *ESL course advice*. Melbourne, Australia: Department of Education.

Board of Studies. (2000a). *The curriculum and standards framework* (2nd ed.). Melbourne, Australia: Author.

Board of Studies. (2000b). *The ESL companion to the English curriculum and standards framework* (2nd ed.). Melbourne, Australia: Author.

Bosher, S. (1992, February). *Evaluation of English as a foreign/second language programs*. Unpublished External Program Review. University of Wisconsin-Eau Claire.

Bourne, J. (1997). "The grown-ups know best": Language policy-making in Britain in the 1990s. In W. Eggington & H. Wren (Eds.), *Language policy: Dominant English, pluralist challenges* (pp. 49–65). Canberra, Australia: John Benjamins.

Brinton, D., Snow, M., & Wesche, M. (1989). *Content-based second language instruction*. Boston: Heinle & Heinle.

Campbell, W. J., & McMeniman, M. (1985). *Bridging the language gap: Ideals and realities pertaining to learning English as a second language (ESL)*. Canberra, Australia: Commonwealth Schools Commission.

Carreathers, K. R., Beekman, L., Coatie, R., & Nelson, W. (1996). Three exemplary retention programs. In I. H. Johnson & A. J. Ottens (Eds.), *Leveling the playing field: Promoting academic success for students of color* (pp. 35–52). San Francisco: Jossey-Bass.

Castles, S., Kalantzis, M., & Cope, B. (1986, October). The end of multiculturalism? *Australian Society*, 3–7.

Catholic Education Office (Victoria). (1990). *Writing in subject areas*. Melbourne, Australia: Author.

Chamot, A., & O'Malley, J. (1987). The cognitive academic language learning approach: A bridge to the mainstream. *TESOL Quarterly, 19*, 227–249.

Christison, M. A., & Krahnke, K. J. (1986). Student perceptions of academic language study. *TESOL Quarterly, 20*, 61–79.

City University of New York. Office of University Relations. (1994). *Investing in the future: A report on the economic impact of the City University of New York*. New York: Author.

Clegg, J. (Ed.). (1996). *Mainstreaming ESL: Case studies in integrating ESL students into the mainstream curriculum*. Clevedon, England: Multilingual Matters.

Cleland, B., & Evans, R. (1984). *ESL topic books: Learning English through general science*. Melbourne, Australia: Longman Cheshire.

Cleland, B., & Evans, R. (1985). *ESL topic books: Learning English through topics about Australia*. Melbourne, Australia: Longman Cheshire.

Cleland, B., & Evans, R. (1988). *ESL topic books: Learning English through topics about Asia*. Melbourne, Australia: Longman Cheshire.

Cochran, E. P. (Ed.). (1992). *Into the academic mainstream: Guidelines for teaching language minority students*. New York: Instructional Resource Center, Office of Academic Affairs, City University of New York.

Cochran, E. P. (1998–1999, Winter). A sociolinguistic typology of learners of English as a second language: What colleges need to know about their international students. *The Ram's Horn, 8*, 24–27.

Commission on Higher Education of the Middle States Association of Colleges and Schools. (1994). *Characteristics of excellence in higher education: Standards for accreditation*. Philadelphia: Author.

Commission on Higher Education of the Middle States Association of Colleges and Schools. (1996). *Framework for outcomes assessment*. Philadelphia: Author.

Cooper, L. O. (1997). Listening competency in the workplace: A model for training. *Business Communication Quarterly, 60*(4), 75–84.

Crandall, J. (1992). Content centered learning in the United States. *Annual Review of Applied Linguistics, 13,* 111–126.

Cronin, M. W., & Ton, H. (1991). Teaching marketing research as an oral communication-intensive course. *Bulletin of the Association for Business Communication, 54*(3), 78–82.

Cummins, J. (1984a). *Bilingualism and special education: Issues in assessment and pedagogy.* San Diego, CA: College-Hill.

Cummins, J. (1984b). Wanted: A theoretical framework for relating language proficiency to academic achievement among bilingual students. In C. Rivera (Ed.), *Language proficiency and academic achievement* (pp. 2–19). Clevedon, England: Multilingual Matters.

Dauer, R. M. (1993). *Accurate English: A complete course in pronunciation.* Englewood Cliffs, NJ: Prentice Hall Regents.

Davis, T. M. (Ed.). (1999). *Open doors 1997/98: Report on international educational exchange.* New York: Institute of International Education.

Davison, C. (1992). Look out! Eight fatal flaws in team and support teaching. *TESOL in Context, 2*(1), 9–10.

Davison, C. (2001). Current policies, programs and practices in school ESL. In B. Mohan, C. Leung, & C. Davison (Eds.), *English as a second language in the mainstream: Teaching, learning and identity* (pp. 30–50). London: Pearson Longman.

Derewianka, B., & Hammond, J. (1991). The pre-service preparation of teachers of students of non-English speaking background. In F. Christie, P. Freebody, A. Devlin, A. Luke, J. Martin, T. Threadgold, & C. Walton (Eds.), *Teaching English literacy: A project of national significance on the preservice preparation of teachers for teaching English literacy* (Vol. 3, pp. 28–68). Darwin, Australia: Centre for Studies of Language in Education, Northern Territory University.

Echevarria, J., Vogt, M., & Short, D. (2000). *Making content comprehensible for English language learners.* Boston: Allyn & Bacon.

Educational Testing Service. (1992). *TOEFL test and score manual.* Princeton, NJ: Author.

Educational Testing Service. (1996). *SPEAK test.* (Available from the Educational Testing Service, P.O. Box 6157, Princeton, NJ 08541)

Education Department of South Australia. (1991). *ESL in the mainstream, Workshops 1–5.* Adelaide, Australia: Government Printer.

Erwin, T. (1991). *Assessing student learning and development: A guide to the principles, goals, and methods of determining college outcomes.* San Francisco, CA: Jossey-Bass.

Ferguson, T. (1991). What's so special about TESOL anyway? *TESOL in Context, 1*(1), 5–7.

Ferris, D., & Tagg, T. (1996). Academic oral communication needs of EAP learners: What subject-matter instructors actually require. *TESOL Quarterly, 30,* 31–55.

Fillmore, L. W. (2000). Loss of family languages: Should educators be concerned? *Theory Into Practice, 39,* 203–210.

Fullan, G. G. (1991). *The new meaning of educational change.* London, England: Cassell.

Gaies, S. (1991). ESL students in academic courses: Forging a link. *College ESL, 1*(1), 30–36.

Gareis, E. (1998). *Guidelines for public speaking.* Unpublished manuscript.

Gareis, E. (1999). [Oral communication in intensive English, college-level ESL, and teacher training programs]. Unpublished raw data.

Grey, M. (1997, Winter). Meatpacking and the migration of immigrants and refugees to the rural midwest. *MidTESOL Newsletter, 18*(4), pp. 1, 3–4.

Griffin, J. H. (1960). *Black like me.* New York: Signet.

Guyer, E., & Peterson, P. W. (1988). Language and/or content? Principles and procedures for materials development in an adjunct course. In S. Benesch (Ed.), *Ending remediation: ESL and content in higher education* (pp. 91–111). Washington, DC: TESOL.

Hagge-Greenberg, L. (1979). *Report on the Liberal Arts Employer Survey: Opportunities for the liberal arts graduate.* Midwest College Placement Association.

Halsell, G. (1996). *In their shoes*. Fort Worth: Texas Christian University Press.

Harrè, R., & Van Langenhove, L. (1999). The dynamics of social episodes. In R. Harrè & L. Van Langenhove (Eds.), *Positioning theory: Moral contexts of intentional action* (pp. 1–13). London: Blackwell.

Henning, G., & Cascallar, E. (1992, February). *A preliminary study of the nature of communicative competence* (Research Report No. 36). Princeton, NJ: Educational Testing Service.

Herriman, M. (1991). *An evaluative study of the Commonwealth ESL program*. Unpublished report for the Department of Employment, Education and Training, Canberra, Australia.

Hill, J., & Hawk, K. (1999). How to understand and better meet the needs of Pacific Island and Maori students. *Education Horizons, 5,* 32–34, 40.

Hill, W. M. F. (1982). *Learning thru discussion*. Beverly Hills, CA: Sage.

Hisrich, J., Upton, T., & Stoffers, P. (1994). Developing English language proficiency among U.S. students of color from second-language backgrounds. West Central Wisconsin Consortium Grant Proposal, University of Wisconsin-Eau Claire.

Hofstede, G. (1997). *Culture and organizations: Software of the mind*. New York: McGraw Hill.

Horowitz, D. M. (1986). What professors actually require: Academic tasks for the ESL classroom. *TESOL Quarterly, 20,* 445–462.

Huffman, W. E., & Miranowski, J. A. (1996). *Immigration, meat packing and trade: Implications for Iowa*. Unpublished manuscript, Iowa State University.

Institute of International Education. (1997). *English language and orientation programs in the United States* (11th ed.). New York: Author.

Internet Resources for Higher Education Outcomes Assessment (n.d.). Retrieved May 24, 2002, from http://www2.acs.ncsu.edu/UPA/assmt/resource.htm

Isonio, S. (1994). *Retention and success rates by course category, year and selected student characteristics at Golden West College*. (ERIC Document Reproduction Service No. ED 377895)

Isonio, S., & Cooperman, C. (1992). *Relationship between grades in speech communication 100 and eligibility for various English writing courses*. (ERIC Document Reproduction Service No. ED 345 785)

Jankovich, J. L., & Powell, K. S. (1997). An implementation model for a communication across the curriculum program. *Business Communication Quarterly, 60*(2), 9–19.

Johns, A. M. (1981). Necessary English: A faculty survey. *TESOL Quarterly, 15,* 51–57.

Jones, L., & von Baeyer, C. (1983). *Functions of American English: Communication activities for the classroom*. New York: Cambridge University Press.

Kaplan, R. B. (1966). Cultural thought patterns in intercultural education. *Language Learning, 16,* 1–20.

Kapoor, S., & Smith, R. (1978, August). *The role of communication in acculturation of foreign students*. Paper presented at the annual meeting of the Association for Education in Journalism, Seattle, WA. (ERIC Document Reproduction Service No. ED 165 183)

Kasper, L. F., et al. (2000). *Content-based college ESL instruction*. Mahwah, NJ: Lawrence Erlbaum.

Kay, A. (1991). The ESL in the mainstream course. *TESOL in Context, 1*(1), 5–7.

Kennedy, S., & Dewar, S. (1997). *Non-English-speaking background students: A study of programmes and supporting New Zealand schools*. Wellington, New Zealand: Ministry of Education.

King, S. (1996). *The green mile*. New York: Simon & Schuster.

Knight, M. (1999). Writing and other communication standards in undergraduate business education: A study of current program requirements, practices, and trends. *Business Communication Quarterly, 62*(1), 10–28.

Krugel, M. L. (1997). Integrating communication in the MBA curriculum. *The Journal of Language for International Business, 8*(2), 36–46.

Let's go! Interactive [Computer software]. (1995). Foster City, CA: DynEd International.

Levin, M. E., & Levin, J. R. (1991). A critical examination of academic retention programs for at-risk minority college students. *Journal of College Student Development, 32,* 323–334.

Levine, D. R., & Adelman, M. B. (1982). *Beyond language: Intercultural communication for English as a second language.* Englewood Cliffs, NJ: Prentice Hall Regents.

Levitz, R., & Noel, L. (1995, July). The earth-shaking but quiet revolution in retention management. (Noel-Levitz Occasional Paper). Iowa City, IA: USA GROUP/Noel-Levitz.

Lo Bianco, J., Liddicoat, A. J., & Crozet, C. (1999). *Striving for the third place: Intercultural competence through language education.* Melbourne: Language Australia.

Maes, J. D., Weldy, T. G., & Icenogle, M. L. (1997). A managerial perspective: Oral communication competency is most important for business students in the workplace. *The Journal of Business Communication, 34*(1), 67–80.

Maher, F. (1985). Classroom pedagogy and the new scholarship on women. In M. Culley & C. Portuges (Eds.), *Gendered subjects: The dynamics of feminist teaching* (pp. 29–48). Boston: Routledge & Kegan Paul.

Mason, A. (1995). By dint of: Student and lecturer perceptions of lecture comprehension strategies in first term graduate study. In J. Flowerdew (Ed.), *Academic listening* (pp. 199–219). Cambridge: Cambridge University Press.

McAuley High School. (n.d.). *Prospectus* (Looseleaf folder). Auckland, New Zealand: Author.

McClean, V. (Ed.). (1999). *Solutions for the new millennium: Race, class, and gender.* Dubuque, IA: Kendall/Hunt.

McClean, V., & Lyles, L. (Eds.). (1993). *Solutions to problems of race, class and gender.* Dubuque, IA: Kendall/Hunt.

McClure, K. (1996). *Putting it together: A conversation management text.* Upper Saddle River, NJ: Prentice Hall Regents.

McKay, P., & Scarino, A. (1991). *The ESL framework of stages.* Melbourne, Australia: Curriculum Corporation.

McNairy, F. G. (1996). The challenge for higher education: Retaining students of color. In I. H. Johnson & A. J. Ottens (Eds.), *Leveling the playing field: Promoting academic success for students of color* (pp. 3–14). San Francisco: Jossey-Bass.

Ministry of Education (Victoria). (1987). *The teaching of English as a second language (ESL): Guidelines for primary and post-primary schools.* Melbourne, Australia: Author.

Ministry of Education. (1988). *Teaching English as a second language: A support document for the English Language Framework.* Melbourne, Australia: Author.

Ministry of Education. (1993). *The New Zealand Curriculum Framework.* Wellington, New Zealand: Author.

Ministry of Education. (1998). *ESOL resourcing information.* Wellington, New Zealand: Author.

Mohan, B. (1986). *Language and content.* Reading, MA: Addison-Wesley.

New York State Education Department, Office of Higher Education. (1996). *Performance reporting in higher education in the nation and New York State: Briefing paper for the Regents Committee on Higher and Professional Education.* Retrieved February 26, 2002, from http://www.highered.nysed.gov/oris/p_report.htm

Nichols, J. (1995). *The departmental guide and record book for student outcomes assessment and institutional effectiveness.* Edison, NJ: Agathon Press.

Nicosa, G. (1997). Implementing public speaking skills across the curriculum. *Community Review, 15,* 75–80.

Nunan, D. (1992). *Research methods in language learning.* Cambridge: Cambridge University Press.

Olsen, R. E. (1993, March). A survey of LEP and adult ESL enrollments in U.S. public schools: Language minority student enrollment data. Symposium conducted at the 27th Annual TESOL Convention, Atlanta, GA.

Oshima, A., & Hogue, A. (1999). *Writing academic English* (3rd ed.). Reading, MA: Addison Wesley Longman.

Ostler, S. E. (1980). A survey of academic needs for advanced ESL. *TESOL Quarterly, 14,* 489–502.

Patkowski, M. (1991). Predictors of college success beyond ESL. In S. Ast (Ed.), *Practical research 3: Studies in academic achievement* (pp. 5–23). New York: Office of Special Programs, The City University of New York.

Patkowski, M., Fox, L., & Smodlaka, I. (1997). Grades of ESL and non-ESL students in selected courses at ten CUNY colleges. *College ESL, 7*(1), 1–13.

Porter, K. (1998, Summer). Growing diversity. *Courier On-Line.* Retrieved May 5, 2001, from http://www.stanleyfoundation.org/courier/articles/1998summer4.html

Powers, D. E. (1986). Academic demands related to listening skills. *Language Testing, 3,* 1–38.

Quirk, R., et al. (Eds.). (1987). *Longman dictionary of contemporary English* (new ed.). Essex, England: Longman Group UK.

Reinsch, N. L., & Shelby, A. N. (1997). What communication abilities do practitioners need? Evidence from MBA students. *Business Communication Quarterly, 60*(4), 7–29.

Reppy, J. M., & Adames, J. (2000). English as a second language: Past, present, and future. In J. W. Rosenthal (Ed.), *Handbook of undergraduate second language education* (pp. 73–92). Mahwah, NJ: Erlbaum.

Richard-Amato, P. (1992). *The multicultural classroom.* New York: Longman.

Robyak, J. E., & Patton, M. J. (1977). The effectiveness of a study skills course for students of different personality types. *Journal of Counseling Psychology, 24,* 200–207.

Romano, J. (1993, September 12). Sex harassment on the job now easier to prove. *The New York Times,* p. NJ1.

Rosenthal, J. W. (1992). A successful transition: A bridge program between ESL and the mainstream classroom. *College Teaching, 40,* 63–66.

Rosenthal, J. W. (1996). *Teaching science to language minority students.* Clevedon, England: Multilingual Matters.

Rosenthal, J. W. (1997). Science students who are still learning English. In P. Alexander, I. Estrada, B. R. Heller, & P. Trotman Reid (Eds.), *Before the class: A handbook for the novice college instructor* (pp. 150–160). New York: CUNY Graduate Center.

Rosenthal, J. W. (2000a). ESL students in the mainstream: Observations from content area faculty. In L. F. Kasper et al., *Content-based college ESL instruction* (pp. 71–90). Mahwah, NJ: Erlbaum.

Rosenthal, J. W. (2000b). Bilingual (dual language) programs: Past, present, and future. In J. W. Rosenthal (Ed.), *Handbook of undergraduate second language education* (pp. 93–113). Mahwah, NJ: Erlbaum.

Rothenberg, P. S. (Ed.). (1998). *Race, class, and gender in the United States: An integrated study.* New York: St. Martin's Press.

Rowe, R. (1999, July 23). Aiming for lift-off. *New Zealand Education Review,* p. 16.

Russikoff, K. A. (1996). *What content faculty really expect of ESL writers.* Paper presented at the 30th Annual TESOL Convention, Chicago, IL.

Santos, T. (1988). Professors' reactions to the academic writing of nonnative-speaking students. *TESOL Quarterly, 22,* 69–90.

Schilling, K., & Schilling, K. (1998). *Proclaiming and sustaining excellence: Assessment as a faculty role.* ASHE-ERIC Higher Education Reports, Vol. 26(3).

Schmidt, B., Badillo, H., Brady, J., MacDonald, H., Ohrenstein, M., Roberts, R., et al. (1999, July 7). *The City University of New York: An institution adrift.* Report of the Mayor's Advisory Task Force on the City University of New York. Retrieved February 8, 2002, from http://www.nyc.gov/html/cuny/home.html

Schneider, A. (1999, March 26). Taking aim at student incoherence. *The Chronicle of Higher Education*, A17.

Sheorey, R., Mokhtari, K., & Livingston, G. (1995). A comparison of native and nonnative English speaking students as college readers. *The Canadian Modern Language Review/La Revue canadiene des langues vivantes, 51*, 661–677.

Skillman, P., & McMahill, C. (1996). *Springboard to success: Communication strategies for the classroom and beyond.* Upper Saddle River, NJ: Prentice Hall Regents.

Smoke, T. (1988). Using feedback from ESL students to enhance their success in college. In S. Benesch (Ed.), *Ending remediation: Linking ESL and content in higher education* (pp. 7–19). Washington, DC: TESOL.

Snow, M. A. (1997). Teaching academic literacy skills: Discipline faculty take responsibility. In D. Brinton & M. A. Snow (Eds.), *The content-based classroom: Perspectives on integrating language and content* (pp. 290–304). White Plains, NY: Longman.

Snow, M. A., & Brinton, D. (1988). The adjunct model of language instruction: An ideal EAP framework. In S. Benesch (Ed.), *Ending remediation: Linking ESL and content in higher education* (pp. 33–52). Washington, DC: TESOL.

Snow, M. A., & Kamhi-Stein, L. D. (1998). Teaching academic literacy skills: A new twist on the adjunct model. *Journal of Intensive English Studies, 1*, 93–108.

Snow, M., Met, M., & Genesee, F. (1989). A conceptual framework for the integration of language and content in second/foreign language instruction. *TESOL Quarterly, 23*, 201–217.

Stake, R. E. (1995). *The art of case study research.* Thousand Oaks, CA: Sage.

Stanton, J. (1997a, December 14). A new life. *Cedar Falls-Waterloo Courier*, pp. 1, A10.

Stanton, J. (1997b, December 14). Refugees stress already tight school budget. *Cedar Falls-Waterloo Courier*, pp. 1, A10.

States mount retention effort. (1994, October). *On Campus, 14*(2), 3.

Steinbach, S. (Producer/Director). (1996). *Fluent American English* [Video series]. (Available from The Seabright Group, 216 F Street, Suite 25, Davis, CA 95616)

Tan, A. (1989). *The joy luck club.* New York: Putnam's.

Tarvers, J. K. (1992). *Women and men.* New York: HarperCollins.

Teays, W. (1996). *Second thoughts: Critical thinking from a multicultural perspective.* Mountain View, CA: Mayfield Publishing.

Tinto, V., Love, G., & Russo, P. (1993). Building community. *Liberal Education, 79*(4), 16–21.

Tinto, V., Love, G., & Russo, P. (1994). *Building learning communities for new college students: A summary of research findings of the Collaborative Learning Project.* University Park, PA: Penn State University, National Center on Postsecondary Teaching, Learning, and Assessment.

Tsui, C. (1992). Teaching EFL industry professionals to make oral presentations in English. *TESOL Journal, 1*(3), 19–22.

U.S. Census Bureau. (2000). U.S. census 2000. Retrieved January 28, 2002, from http://www.dhs.state.ia.us/Homepages/dhs/refugee/IowaRefugeePopulation.htm

Valentine, J. F., & Repath-Martos, L. M. (1997). How relevant is relevant? In M. A. Snow & D. M. Brinton (Eds.), *The content-based classroom* (pp. 233–247). White Plains, NY: Addison Wesley Longman.

Vann, R., Lorenz, F. O., & Meyer, D. M. (1991). Error gravity: Faculty response to errors in the written discourse of nonnative speakers of English. In L. Hamp-Lyons (Ed.), *Assessing second language writing in academic contexts* (pp. 181–196). Norwood, NJ: Ablex.

Vann, R. J., Meyer, D. M., & Lorenz, F. O. (1984). Error gravity: A study of faculty opinion of ESL errors. *TESOL Quarterly, 18*, 427–440.

Waner, K. K. (1995). Business communication competencies needed by employees as perceived by business faculty and business professionals. *Business Communication Quarterly, 58*(4), 51–56.

Wanning, E. (1997). *Culture shock! USA.* Portland, OR: Graphic Arts Center Publishing Company.

Yin, R. K. (1994). *Case study research: Design and methods* (2nd ed.). Thousand Oaks, CA: Sage.

Youngs, C. S., & Youngs, G. A., Jr. (2001). Predictors of mainstream teachers' attitudes toward ESL students. *TESOL Quarterly, 35,* 97–120.

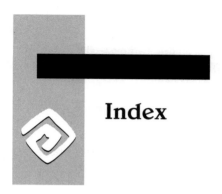

Index

Page numbers followed by *f* and *t* indicate figures and tables, respectively.

Also Available From TESOL

Academic Writing Programs
Ilona Leki, Editor

Action Research
Julian Edge, Editor

Bilingual Education
Donna Christian and Fred Genesee, Editors

CALL Environments:
Research, Practice, and Critical Issues
Joy Egbert and Elizabeth Hanson-Smith, Editors

Community Partnerships
Elsa Auerbach, Editor

Distance-Learning Programs
Lynn E. Henrichsen, Editor

Implementing the ESL Standards for Pre-K–12 Students Through Teacher Education
Marguerite Ann Snow, Editor

Integrating the ESL Standards Into Classroom Practice: Grades Pre-K–2
Betty Ansin Smallwood, Editor

Integrating the ESL Standards Into Classroom Practice: Grades 3–5
Katharine Davies Samway, Editor

Integrating the ESL Standards Into Classroom Practice: Grades 6–8
Suzanne Irujo, Editor

Integrating the ESL Standards Into Classroom Practice: Grades 9–12
Barbara Agor, Editor

Intensive English Programs in Postsecondary Settings
Nicholas Dimmitt and Maria Dantas-Whitney, Editors

Internet for English Teaching
Mark Warschauer, Heidi Shetzer, and Christine Meloni

Journal Writing
Jill Burton and Michael Carroll, Editors

Managing ESL Programs in Rural and Small Urban Schools
Barney Bérubé

Reading and Writing in More Than One Language:
Lessons for Teachers
Elizabeth Franklin, Editor

Teacher Education
Karen E. Johnson, Editor

Teaching in Action: Case Studies From Second Language Classrooms
Jack C. Richards, Editor

Technology-Enhanced Learning Environments
Elizabeth Hanson-Smith, Editor

For more information, contact
Teachers of English to Speakers of Other Languages, Inc.
700 South Washington Street, Suite 200
Alexandria, Virginia 22314 USA
Tel 703-836-0774 • Fax 703-836-6447 • publications@tesol.org •
http://www.tesol.org/